Teachers voyaging in plurilingual seas:
Young children learning through more
than one language

Teachers voyaging in plurilingual seas: Young children learning through more than one language

Valerie N. Podmore, Helen Hedges, Peter J. Keegan and Nola Harvey (Editors)

NZCER PRESS

NZCER PRESS
New Zealand Council for Educational Research
PO Box 3237
Wellington
New Zealand

© Authors, 2016

ISBN 978-1-927231-98-2

No part of the publication may be copied, stored or communicated in any form by any means (paper or digital), including recording or storing in an electronic retrieval system, without the written permission of the publisher.
Education institutions that hold a current licence with Copyright Licensing New Zealand may copy from this book in strict accordance with the terms of the CLNZ Licence.

A catalogue record for this book is available from the National Library of New Zealand

Designed by Smartwork Creative Ltd, www.smartworkcreative.co.nz

Contents

Foreword	vii
Preface	xiii
Chapter 1 Introduction: Scanning policy and curriculum horizons Valerie N. Podmore, Nola Harvey, Helen Hedges and Peter J. Keegan	1
Chapter 2 Language diversity in context: Navigation points Nola Harvey, Helen Hedges and Valerie N. Podmore	12
Chapter 3 Researching language diversity: Charting procedures Peter J. Keegan, Valerie N. Podmore, Nola Harvey and Helen Hedges	30
Chapter 4 Te Puna Kōhungahunga Jasmine Castle, Marama Young, Karen Liley, Peter J. Keegan and Tania Popata	45
Chapter 5 The A'oga Fa'a Samoa: A Samoan-immersion centre Eneleata Tapusoa, Valerie N. Podmore, Patisepa Tuafuti, Jan Taouma and May Crichton	57
Chapter 6 Multilingual children, multilingual teachers: Symonds Street Early Childhood Education Centre Thirumagal Anandh, Nola Harvey and Helen Hedges; with Auemetua Lotomau and Ruwinaaz Subhani	79
Chapter 7 Multilingual children, monolingual teachers: Mangere Bridge Kindergarten Carol Hartley, Pat Rogers, Jemma Smith and Daniel Lovatt; with Nola Harvey and Helen Hedges	98
Chapter 8 Conclusions: Insightful landings Nola Harvey, Helen Hedges, Valerie N. Podmore and Peter J. Keegan	116
Appendix A 'The child's questions': Questions for teachers of children who learn in more than one language	134
Appendix B Questions for teachers to support the learning of children who learn in more than one language	136
Acknowledgements	138
Index	139

Foreword

The principal message of this book is the key importance to bi/multilingual children's lives of the use of their heritage/home language for learning in early childhood education. A central theme is that the multiple languages that children and their families bring to early childhood settings can be fostered and validated through intentional planning and innovative pedagogies, practices and policies. The metaphor used as the title of this book skilfully draws our attention to the uncharted waters in early childhood education where many children in Aotearoa New Zealand from bi/multilingual backgrounds learn through their languages in plurilingual contexts. The book's unique focus on children from birth to 5 years is a significant contribution to the field of early childhood education as the emphasis is placed on young children's learning experiences in more than one language.

In many super-diverse nation states such as Canada, the US, Australia, India and Aotearoa New Zealand, plurilingualism and linguistic diversity are characterised by varieties of cultural and linguistic practices that operate simultaneously in contexts of post colonialism and immigration within an indigenous presence. Transmigration, global fluidity of labour markets, rapid change, advanced technologies and media communications facilitated by globalisation have altered the varieties of social, cultural, and linguistic diversity inherent in super-diverse post-multicultural societies (Jones Díaz, 2016; Vertovec, 2007). Therefore, the combination of globalisation and super diversity has resulted in the existence of super-diverse nation states such as Aotearoa New Zealand.

The study reported in this book respectfully documents bi/multilingual children's experiences with their languages, families' concerns for their children's bi/multilingual trajectory, and educational implications that foster and validate children's heritage/home languages in early childhood settings, in the family and in the community. Innovative pedagogical strategies are offered for providing opportunities for bi/multilingual children to use and learn in their heritage/

home languages, which are informed by the broader principles, aspirations and goals of *Te Whāriki*—Aotearoa New Zealand's national early childhood curriculum.

An innovative approach in the methodology of the study is the documentation of the ways in which four uniquely different early childhood settings engaged in opportunities and addressed challenges in promoting and extending children's heritage/home languages, including te reo Māori, Pasifika languages and immigrant community languages. The findings reported from this important study are resourcefully written by teacher–researchers who worked collaboratively with university researchers.

Studies that specifically investigate young children's experiences of learning in more than one language in early childhood education and growing up bi/multilingual are scant, particularly in the Australasia, Asia and the Pacific Islands. Furthermore, there are gaps in the research literature documenting the impact of the broader social structures and processes of language loss/shift in children, driven by English-only educational policies and pedagogies. This scarcity of research has produced a number of silences in bi/multilingual children's capacity to retain their heritage/home languages when attending early childhood settings (Jones Díaz, 2015). In my research, it was apparent that parents had few opportunities to share their concerns or engage in conversations with educators about their children's bi/multilingual experiences (Jones Díaz, 2007). Parents are often hesitant to report that they speak more than one language at home, for fear that educators will judge them for doing the wrong thing by their children. Moreover, normative monolingual English-only attitudes expressed by community members, teachers and other professionals can pressure bi/multilingual families into abandoning the heritage/home language. This can also be driven by misguided fears and myths that speaking more than one language at home is an impediment to their children's English language learning (Jones Díaz, 2014; Schwartz, 2010). Equally, early childhood educators can often feel that they lack the confidence and expertise to address such matters with parents and as a result avoid having such conversations with them. The findings presented in this book refreshingly document positive outcomes, when educators communicate with families about their children's bi/multilingual trajectory. This provides a significant contribution to addressing the scarcity of research literature in bi/multilingual early childhood education. Importantly, the educators' reflections on their experiences working with bi/multilingual families offer crucial insights for all educators working in linguistically and culturally diverse educational settings.

Throughout history, in many countries, children's use of their heritage/home languages in educational settings has often been systematically silenced, explicitly excluded, aggressively forbidden and overtly sanctioned as deviant behaviour. This has institutionally reinforced the sole use and normalisation of official languages, such as English, French and Japanese (to name a few) (Liddicoat & Curnow, 2014). Such historical rationalist nation-building agendas emphasised models of monolingualism, in which linguistic diversity was considered a threat to national cohesion. The education of children was the vehicle for establishing national identity and the nation state, which in turn constructed a monolingual conceptualization of the school (Liddicoat & Curnow, 2014). Unfortunately, many educational institutions today, including early childhood education, have inherited such monolingual models, resulting in the privileging of official languages at the expense of indigenous and immigrant/community languages. Even today, throughout much of the English-speaking world and in Europe, children's heritage/home languages are often dismissed or ignored (Gogolin, 2011). The findings reported in this work highlight the crucial role heritage/home languages play in young children's lives and provide new models of multilingualism and plurilingualism that can be adopted in early childhood education.

On a global and local scale, concerns for the disappearance of indigenous languages and non-global languages pose a severe threat to the diversity of cultures, identities and knowledges that exist in the world (Jones Díaz, 2016). Linguists have predicted that of the 7000 languages spoken throughout the world, by the next century half will be extinct (Russ, 2012). In postcolonial nation states such as Aotearoa New Zealand, Australia, and countries within Latin America, Asia, Europe and Africa with an indigenous presence, issues of language revival and retention are of major concern for indigenous communities, families and indigenous educators and non-indigenous educators alike. Therefore intergenerational language retention is the key to ensuring that indigenous bi/multilingual children have access to quality educational programmes that facilitate and foster their languages in order to maximise their linguistic, cultural and social potential. As early childhood educators are often the frontline workers for indigenous and immigrant families, they have a responsibility to ensure that their pedagogical practices do not inhibit or prohibit children's use of their languages for learning. This book details useful strategies for representing and incorporating the languages and cultural practices of children and their families into the curriculum, particularly in settings where there are many languages and dialects spoken.

Discourses of deficit, often applied to indigenous communities and extended to immigrant bi/multilingual communities, often permeate many educators' expectations of bi/multilingual children where low expectations of their intellectual and linguistic potential position them as less capable than their English-speaking monolingual peers. In the case of Aotearoa New Zealand, where deficit views of Māori and Pasifika children's achievement have persisted, this book draws on enriched theoretical perspectives which frame a credit-based view of bi/multilingual children and families to inform policy and pedagogy. This permits a pedagogically active responsiveness to children's multiple languages and diverse cultural practices.

Therefore the pedagogical and political implications for young bi/multilingual children and their families cannot be ignored. Unless bi/multilingual children have opportunities to learn in their heritage/home languages they are denied their rights that are at the centre of a democratic education. This book alerts us to these rights, through a candid reminder of the United Nations Convention on the Rights of the Child (United Nations, 1989) and in the United Nations Declaration on the Rights of Indigenous Peoples (United Nations, 2008) which outline their rights to the protection of indigenous languages such as te reo Māori, and other heritage/home languages including immigrant community languages and New Zealand Sign Language (NZSL). Therefore the message is clear and explicit: early childhood education has a significant responsibility to ensure that all children have the right to learn in their language/s to enable them to take full advantage of their social, cultural, linguistic and intellectual assets.

In their work as early childhood educators, academics and researchers, the authors of this book have successfully offered new insights into a diversity of pedagogical practices that positively promote learning in more than one language in Aotearoa New Zealand. These practices are informed credit-based theoretical approaches and the multiple voices of children, parents and educators that participated in the study. This work brings to readers passion, insights into and commitment towards achieving linguistic equality in the context of learning for bi/multilingual children and their families in early childhood education.

Dr. Criss Jones Díaz
Centre for Educational Research
Western Sydney University

References

Goglin, I. (2011). The challenge for superdiversity for education in Europe. *Education Enquiry, 2*(2), 239–249.

Jones Díaz, C. (2007). *Intersections between language retention and identities in young bilingual children*. Unpublished PhD dissertation, University of Western Sydney: Sydney, NSW.

Jones Díaz, C. (2014). Languages and literacies in childhood bilingualism: Building on cultural and linguistic capital in early childhood education. In L. Arthur, J. Ashton, & B. Beecher (Eds.), *Diverse literacies in early childhood: A social justice approach* (pp. 106–125). Camberwell, VIC: Australian Council for Educational Research.

Jones Díaz, C. (2015). Silences in growing up bilingual in multicultural globalised societies: Educators', families' and children's views of negotiating languages, identity and difference in childhood. In T. Ferfolja, C. Jones Díaz & J. Ullman (Eds.), *Understanding sociological theory and pedagogical practices* (pp. 110–128). Cambridge: Cambridge University Press.

Jones Díaz, C. (2016). Growing up bilingual and negotiating identity in globalised and multicultural Australia: Exploring transformations and contestations of identity and bilingualism in contexts of hybridity and diaspora. In D. Cole & C. Woodrow (Eds.), *Superdimensions in globalisation and education*. Springer: Singapore.

Liddicoat, A. J. & Curnow, T. J. (2014). Students' home languages and the struggle for space in the curriculum, *International Journal of Multilingualism, 11*(3), 273–288, doi: 10. 1080/14790718.2014.921175.

Russ, R. (2012). Vanishing voices. *National Geographic*, (July 2012): 60–87.

Schwartz, M. (2010). Family language policy: Core issues of an emerging field *Applied Linguistics Review*. (1), 171–192, doi: 10.1515/9783110222654.171

Vertovec, S. (2007). Super-diversity and its implications. *Ethnic and Racial Studies, 30*(6), 1024–1054.

Preface

Toi te reo, toi te tangata, toi te mana.
Protect the language, the people, the mana.

This book launches us into previously uncharted waters on the important topic of learning and teaching with young children who learn in more than one language in Aotearoa New Zealand. The book is about young children who learn *through* more than one language—children who experience interactions in languages other than or as well as English at home and/or in early childhood education settings. (This contrasts with the considerable body of previous research about the teaching and learning *of* second or other languages.) The main focus is on children aged from birth to 5 years who attend early childhood education (ECE) centres, their teachers, and their families. The book includes work we completed for a project funded by the Teaching and Learning Research Initiative (TLRI) and provides new insights derived from the findings and the teachers' research experiences.

Background to the TLRI research project and this book

The TLRI acknowledged how important this topic is to teachers when in 2012 they called for research proposals addressing the topic "Supporting learning in the early years for children who learn in more than one language: Developing deeper understandings for practice". Our team of researchers at the University of Auckland, in partnership with four different ECE centres, worked together to prepare and submit a proposal focusing on children who learn in more than one language.

This book draws on our Early Years TLRI project (January 2013–June 2015), which was situated within four diverse ECE settings in the Auckland region. We outline the languages spoken by teachers, parents and children, and place a special focus on the experiences and outcomes that teachers, parents and children value, noting the opportunities and implications for practice.

Outline of the structure of the book

The first three chapters provide the background to the research and explain how credit-based ideas influence the research and its implications for policy and practice. These provide the map we used to explore understanding more about teaching and learning with children who learn in more than one language in Aotearoa New Zealand.

Chapter 1 clarifies the parameters of the project, outlining relevant policy and early childhood curriculum considerations and describing changes in Auckland and Aotearoa New Zealand. It draws on and summarises relevant data from the recent 2013 census, and points to some related trends, challenges and opportunities for early childhood teachers.

Chapter 2 places language diversity in context by reviewing relevant literature and discussing the theoretical framings of the project. Three overarching research questions are presented to guide our research.

Chapter 3 includes an outline of the overall project design, research questions and research processes, with a special focus on challenges for teacher-researchers working with children who learn in more than one language. There is a summary of the quantitative findings across the four diverse ECE centre settings.

The following four chapters are written by teacher-researchers from each of the four ECE centres, working alongside and supported by university researchers. There is a focus on children's, parents' and teachers' journeys within each of the four waka (or centres). The chapters outline the contexts, findings and pedagogical implications from each setting.

Chapter 8, the final chapter, reflects on the principles and theoretical insights across the contexts and preceding chapters, mapping out implications for teachers, families, researchers and policy makers.

How readers might use this book

Chapters 4, 5, 6 and 7 are from four different types of ECE settings. We invite readers to reflect on each of these chapters, then to consider the types of settings that most closely resemble their own experiences. This process offers the opportunity to transfer insights about young children who learn in more than one language to other contexts, nationally and internationally.

Metaphors used in this book

Lastly, Aotearoa New Zealand is an island nation situated between two large oceans. Within this book we have selected metaphors that reflect historical and contemporary challenges and opportunities. These metaphors relate to scanning horizons, navigating and charting oceans, and negotiating landings.

> *Man [sic] cannot discover new oceans unless he has
> the courage to lose sight of the shore. (André Gide)*

Chapter 1 Introduction: Scanning policy and curriculum horizons

Valerie N. Podmore, Nola Harvey, Helen Hedges and Peter J. Keegan

E taea te piki te ngaru o te moana.
The swell of the sea can be overcome.

This whakataukī signals our optimism about launching into uncharted waters to generate new knowledge.

Young children's right to have their heritage/home languages respected in educational settings is enshrined in the United Nations Convention on the Rights of the Child (UNCRC)[1] and in the United Nations Declaration on the Rights of Indigenous Peoples (United Nations, 2008). Aotearoa New Zealand is a signatory to both. Teachers, as duty bearers of children's rights, are able to use the UNCRC as a useful benchmark alongside the principles of *Te Whāriki*, the New Zealand early childhood curriculum (Ministry of Education, 1996). These documents can guide policies that protect, promote and develop an ECE centre's practices and ensure they are responsive to children's use of heritage/home languages.

This chapter provides an overview of policy and curriculum documents relevant to teaching and research with young children who learn in more than one language. We include 2013 census data and related considerations that defined the rationale for, and the parameters of, the present project. Finally, we offer provocations for the trends, challenges and opportunities for teachers as they respond to the increasing diversity of languages used by the children and families with whom they partner in ECE settings.

Policy and curriculum considerations

The UNCRC established human rights standards for the status and treatment of children. As a signatory to the UNCRC, the New Zealand Government is obligated to ensure and protect a child's identity, values and right to use her or his home/heritage languages. The UNCRC states:

> States Parties agree that the education of the child shall be directed to: …(c) The development of respect for the child's parents, his or her own cultural identity, language and values, for the national values of the country in which the child is living, the country from which he or she may originate, and for civilizations different from his or her own. (Article 29[c])

In addition, the UNCRC specifically promotes the protection of indigenous languages:

> In those States in which ethnic, religious or linguistic minorities or persons of indigenous origin exist, a child belonging to such a minority or who is indigenous shall not be denied the right, in community with other members of his or her group, to enjoy his or her own culture, to profess and practise his or her own religion, or to use his or her own language. (Article 30)

Moreover, the UNCRC signals a responsibility to listen to children's views and hear children's voices: "States Parties shall assure the child who is capable of forming his or her own views the right to express those views freely in matters affecting the child" (Article 12, 1).

The United Nations Declaration on the Rights of Indigenous Peoples also sets out obligations for the protection of and provision for indigenous peoples' intergenerational transfer of languages (Article 13.1). This declaration was endorsed by the New Zealand Government in April 2010.

When considering the rights of children who learn in more than one language in Aotearoa New Zealand, the Treaty of Waitangi (Te Tiriti o Waitangi), signed in 1840 by British Crown representative William Hobson and more than 500 Māori chiefs, is an important overarching covenant. Most of the Māori chiefs signed the Treaty document that was written in te reo Māori, which guarantees possession and protection of taonga. In 1986 the Māori Language Board of Wellington pointed out that taonga ("valued customs and possessions") includes te reo Māori (the Māori language) (Orange, 1987, p. 250).

With the passing of the Māori Language Act in August 1987, te reo Māori was finally recognised as an official language of Aotearoa New Zealand, and the Māori Language Commission was set up to promote and supervise te reo Māori (Te Taura Whiri, 2015). Guided by Te Tiriti o Waitangi, and recognising the national status of te reo Māori, we acknowledge that attention to te reo Māori and tikanga Māori is a priority.

Freedom to use other home/heritage languages as well as Aotearoa New Zealand's official languages of English, te reo Māori and New Zealand Sign Language (NZSL) is protected, too, by the New Zealand Bill of Rights Act 1990, according to which, the rights of a minority group include the right to "use the language, of that minority" (Ministry of Justice, 1990, Part 2, Article 20).

However, at present in Aotearoa New Zealand languages other than English, te reo Māori and NZSL have no official status, yet researchers contend that teachers and families have a responsibility to progress opportunities for heritage/home language survival and usage in both home and educational settings (Cummins, 2000; May, 2011). Attempts have been made by the Human Rights Commission (2008) to draft language policies, but these are yet to be made official. The report *Languages in Aotearoa New Zealand* by the Royal Society of New Zealand (2013) made the point that most of the world has always been multilingual and that efforts have been made to promote languages policies elsewhere.

Early childhood education in Aotearoa New Zealand has a history of progressing and negotiating the choppy waters of social justice issues. A current policy goal for ECE is to increase participation (specifically, enrolment numbers) in the diverse range of ECE services present in early childhood services in Aotearoa New Zealand (Meade & Podmore, 2010).

In 2013 the Government specified 10 outcomes the public sector were expected to achieve within 5 years. These included one for ECE, which focused on participation, setting a target that in 2016 "98% of children starting school will have participated in quality ECE" (Ministry of Education, 2015). The State Services Commission reported steady progress towards this target, and that the Ministry of Education was "intensifying engagement with priority communities in order to reach the 98% target in 2016" (State Services Commission, 2015).

This policy goal, alongside rights and Te Tiriti o Waitangi obligations, led us to question how young children who learn in more than one language experience participation in early childhood education. How might Articles 29(c) and 30 of the UNCRC be enacted in early childhood settings? Participation in this sense is a more dynamic concept, drawing on sociocultural and sociological childhood framings (Harvey, 2013).

The aspirations and principles of *Te Whāriki*, the national early childhood curriculum, are paramount considerations when working with young children who learn in more than one language, and their families. *Te Whāriki* is bicultural in both name and emphasis, stating that

> In early childhood education settings, all children should be given the opportunity to develop knowledge and an understanding of the cultural heritages of both partners to Te Tiriti o Waitangi. (Ministry of Education, 1996, p. 9)

Part B of *Te Whāriki* is written in te reo Māori and is specifically designed for Māori-medium services.

The curriculum aspirations for children "to grow up as competent and confident learners and communicators, healthy in mind, body, and spirit, secure in their sense of belonging and in the knowledge that they make a valued contribution to society" (p. 9) emphasise the importance of belonging and identity to infants' and young children's learning. The aims and focus of this study are consistent with, and draw upon, the aspirations, principles and goals of *Te Whāriki*. All strands of the curriculum were relevant to research with children who learn in more than one language. The principles of *empowerment, family and community, relationships,* and *holistic learning and development* provided important navigation points on the horizon to guide this study.

Furthermore, the *Te Whāriki* strand of Communication specifies that children should experience the languages, stories and symbols of their own and other cultures. Within this strand, two learning outcomes are "confidence that their first language is valued" and "an appreciation of te reo as a living and relevant language" (p. 76). Examples of reflective questions include:

> In what ways is Māori language included in the programme? To what extent do adults include phrases from children's home languages when talking with them? ... What opportunities are there for children to hear stories, poems, chants, and songs? How well do these connect to the child's culture? ... How is the use of community languages incorporated into the programme? (Ministry of Education, 1996, p. 76)

Throughout *Te Whāriki*, readers can find similar questions for rich guidance on inclusive practices to support heritage and home languages.

Several policy documents also inform practice by specifying plans for the educational success of Māori and Pasifika[2] learners. *Ka Hikitia: Accelerating Success 2013–2017: The Māori Education Strategy* has the vision of "Māori enjoying and achieving success as Māori" through "an engaging and enjoyable educational journey that recognises and celebrates their unique identity, language and culture" (Ministry of Education, 2013b, p. 13). One of its goals reminds early childhood teachers to encourage participation in and the use of te reo Māori for learning. Another document, *The Pasifika Education Plan 2013–2017*, promotes the vision of all Pasifika children being able to participate, engage and achieve in education "secure in their identities, languages and cultures" (Ministry of Education, 2012, p. 3).

In addition, *The New Zealand Curriculum for English-medium Teaching and Learning in Years 1–13* states that "students' identities, languages, abilities, and talents are recognised and affirmed" (Ministry of Education, 2007, p. 9). This is the curriculum that children go on to experience in schools. It includes the view that Aotearoa New Zealand as a society should be able to engage at least with the multilingual Asia–Pacific region.

We planned this research to understand in greater depth how learning and teaching for young children who learn in more than one language in Aotearoa New Zealand might be recognised and enhanced. The context of the study was Auckland, the largest city in Aotearoa New Zealand and one that has recently been ascribed super-diversity status by the Royal Society of New Zealand (2013), exemplified by recent census data.

Ethnicities and languages: census data

Learners in Aotearoa New Zealand are increasingly likely to speak more than one language. This nationwide trend is most evident in the Auckland region (Statistics New Zealand, 2006, 2013). Initially, data from the 2006 census endorsed the timeliness of the present study, and more recently data from the 2013 census provided further evidence of ethnic and language diversity. Table 1.1 provides data from the 2013 census showing that diversity is particularly evident within the Auckland region. European (Pākehā), Māori, Pasifika and Asian people are the most prevalent groups, with notably high proportions of the country's total Pasifika and Asian people residing in Auckland.

Table 1.1: Ethnicity in New Zealand in 2013

Ethnic group	Auckland		New Zealand		Auckland as a proportion of NZ
	Count	%	Count	%	%
European	789,306	59.3	2,969,391	74.0	26.6
Māori	142,767	10.7	598,602	14.9	23.9
Pacific peoples	194,958	14.6	295,941	7.4	65.9
Asian	307,233	23.1	471,708	11.8	65.1
Middle Eastern / Latin American / African	24,945	1.9	46,956	1.2	53.1
Other	15,639	1.2	67,752	1.7	23.1
Total people specifying ethnicity	1,331,427	110.8*	4,011,402	111.0*	33.2
Not elsewhere included	84,123		230,646		36.5
Total people	1,415,550		4,242,048		33.4

Note:

* Due to multiple identification (individual respondents stating more than one ethnic group) percentages total more than 100 percent.

The languages spoken most widely throughout Aotearoa New Zealand, as recorded in the 2013 census, are: English, Māori, Samoan, Hindi and northern Chinese (Mandarin). In Auckland there is a high concentration of Hindi, Northern Chinese and Samoan speakers (see Table 1.2).

Table 1.2: Top 12 languages spoken in New Zealand in 2013

Language	Auckland		New Zealand		Auckland as a proportion of NZ
	Count	%	Count	%	%
English	1,233,633	95.6	3,819,969	97.8	32.3
Samoan	58,200	4.5	86,406	2.2	67.4
Hindi	49,518	3.8	66,312	1.6	74.7
Northern Chinese	38,781	3.0	52,263	1.3	74.2
Māori	30,927	2.4	148,395	3.8	20.8
Yue	30,681	2.4	44,625	1.1	68.6
Sinitic	30,282	2.3	42,750	1.1	70.8
Tongan	26,028	2.3	31,839	0.8	81.7
Korean	19,365	1.5	26,373	0.7	60.8
French	17,433	1.4	49,125	1.3	35.5
Tagalog	14,925	1.2	29,016	0.7	51.4
Afrikaans	13,992	1.1	27,387	0.7	51.1
Total people stated	1,316,262	134.1*	3,973,359	101.7*	

Note:
* Due to multiple identification (individual respondents stating more than one ethnic group) percentages total more than 100 percent.

Nationally, the number of Hindi speakers increased significantly, and most markedly in Auckland, between the 2006 and 2013 censuses. For example, in 2006 there were 34,614 Hindi speakers in Auckland, but by 2013 there were 49,518, an increase of 43 percent. Of notable concern is a consistent decrease in te reo Māori speakers in over the last decade. The number of te reo Māori speakers fell by 12,132 between 2001 and 2013, with a recent decrease of 8,715 between 2006 and 2013. Given that te reo Māori is the only indigenous language of Aotearoa New Zealand, reversing this trend is an urgent challenge for teachers, families and policy makers.

Trends, challenges and opportunities

The authors of the longitudinal study Growing up in New Zealand, which was based on a sample of households in Auckland, reported additional information about diversity of languages. Morton et al. (2014, p. 52) released findings from parent interviews which indicated that by 2 years of age 2,514 (40 percent) of children understood two or more languages and 431 (7 percent) understood three or more languages. The majority of children—6,090 (96 percent)—understood English; 763 (12 percent) understood te reo Māori; 464 (7 percent) understood Samoan; 302 (5 percent) understood Tongan; and 258 (4 percent) understood Hindi.

Findings specifically for Māori children in the study showed that by age 2 years more Māori children (60 percent) *could not* understand te reo Māori than *could* understand te reo Māori. Consistent with our concerns already expressed, these authors contended that the future of te reo Māori is strongly connected both to the capability of families with infants to speak te reo Māori in their homes, and to the use of te reo Māori within educational and other settings (Growing Up in New Zealand, 2015). These findings offer challenges to early childhood teachers, families, policy makers and researchers.

The Royal Society of New Zealand (RSNZ) highlighted rights and obligations relevant to children and families in their inquiry into the major issues facing language practices given the diversity within New Zealand. The RSNZ identified Auckland as a super-diverse city and made a case for the development of a languages policy as a way to support New Zealand's transition to a multilingual and multi-literate country (Royal Society of New Zealand, 2013). The RSNZ raised questions for policy and practice about who might take up the responsibility, alongside families, to protect and promote a range of languages. Clearly, with a policy emphasis on participation, ECE centres ought to shoulder some of this responsibility. For speakers of minority languages, English-medium settings that require children to leave their home/heritage language at home would offer little in terms of bilingual children's cognitive and language development.

Ways to address the diversity of languages may be over-simplified in some centres' languages policy statement—if they have one—and also in pedagogy. These over-simplifications risk leading to diversity becoming invisible. This was the case with the annual information about children and staff that the Ministry of Education required ECE centres and services to report up until July 2013. These recorded a child's ethnicities but excluded their languages—although teachers were asked to report the languages they used for teaching. Ethnic identity is a broad indicator and may not accurately reflect languages spoken. In this way, the richness of language resources children have for future learning success was not captured or addressed.

Subsequently, from 2014 the Ministry of Education has progressively introduced a new digital data collection procedure for ECE services. This Early Learning Information system (ELI) included the allocation of a National Student Number (NSN) unique to each child, and directed teachers to identify and record the languages spoken in each enrolled child's home (Ministry of Education, 2013a). The ELI continues recording teachers' approximations of their use of te reo Māori, Pasifika and Asian languages in their services. One limitation was that relatively few services were using this system in 2014. However, the ELI questions potentially open up conversations about languages used at home and may act as a prompt for an exchange of information between parents and teachers about home and centre support for bilingualism.

In general, then, ECE statistics are gradually including Māori and Pasifika languages, and more extensive data are being collected. Our current study covered a wide range of languages, including te reo Māori, Pasifika languages, English, and all languages children spoke at home.

Rationale for the study

When we developed this study there was a dearth of detailed, consistent data within and across ECE centres on the languages spoken by children in ECE centres and at home with their families. Given the increasing responsibilities ascribed to ECE centres by policy and curriculum, the issue arose as to what might be considered valued outcomes by teachers and families for children who learn in more than one language.

In summary, this chapter has scanned aspects of the policy and curriculum horizons and presented statistical data on languages and ethnicities that pertain to supporting children who learn in more than one language. The next chapter provides an overview of the literature and theoretical positions that led to the present study and specifies three overarching research questions.

> *If you talk to a man [sic] in a language he understands, that goes to his head. If you talk to him in his language, that goes to his heart.*
> *(Nelson Mandela)*

References

Cummins, J. (2000). *Language, power and pedagogy: Bilingual children in the crossfire.* Clevedon, UK: Multilingual Matters.

Growing up in New Zealand. (2015). *The intergenerational use of te reo Māori: Evidence from Growing up in New Zealand* [Policy Brief 5]. Auckland: Author.

Harvey, N. (2013). Principled practices: Respect and reciprocity through linguistically responsive pedagogy. *Early Childhood Folio, 17*(1), 19–23.

Human Rights Commission. (2008). *Languages in Aotearoa New Zealand te waka reo: Statement on language policy.* Retrieved from https://www.hrc.co.nz/your-rights/race-relations-and-diversity/language/our-work/

May, S. (2011). *Language and minority rights: Ethnicity, nationalism and the politics of language* (2nd ed.). New York, NY: Routledge.

Meade, A., & Podmore, V. N. (2010). *Caring and learning together: A case study of New Zealand.* UNESCO Early Childhood and Family Policy Series No.16—2010. Retrieved from http://unesdoc.unesco.org/images/0018/001872/187234e.pdf

Ministry of Education. (1996). *Te whāriki: He whāriki mātauranga mō ngā mokopuna o Aotearoa: Early childhood curriculum.* Wellington: Learning Media. Retrieved from http://www.education.govt.nz/early-childhood/teaching-and-learning/ece-curriculum/

Ministry of Education. (2007). *The New Zealand curriculum for English-medium teaching and learning in years 1–13.* Retrieved from http://nzcurriculum.tki.org.nz/The-New-Zealand-Curriculum

Ministry of Education. (2012). *The Pasifika education plan 2013–2017.* Retrieved from http://www.education.govt.nz/ministry-of-education/overall-strategies-and-policies/pasifika-education-plan-2013-2017/

Ministry of Education. (2013a). *Early Learning Information system.* Retrieved from http://eli.education.govt.nz/overview/eli-information-collection/

Ministry of Education. (2013b). *Ka hikitia: Accelerating success 2013–2017: The Māori education strategy*. Retrieved from http://www.education.govt.nz/ministry-of-education/overall-strategies-and-policies/the-maori-education-strategy-ka-hikitia-accelerating-success-20132017/

Ministry of Education. (2015). *Current Ministry priorities in early childhood education: Better public services: Results for New Zealanders*. Retrieved from http://www.education.govt.nz/early-childhood/ministry-priorities/

Ministry of Justice. (1990). *New Zealand Bill of Rights, 1990*. Retrieved from http://www.legislation.govt.nz/act/public/1990/0109/latest/DLM224792.html

Morton, S. M. B., Atatoa Carr, P. E., Grant, C. C., Berry, S. D., Bandara, D. K., Mohal, J., et al. (2014). *Growing up in New Zealand: A longitudinal study of New Zealand children and their families: Now we are two: Describing our first 1000 days*. Auckland: Growing Up in New Zealand.

Orange, C. (1987). *The Treaty of Waitangi*. Wellington: Allen & Unwin / Port Nicholson Press.

Royal Society of New Zealand. (2013). *Languages in Aotearoa New Zealand*. Wellington: Author. Retrieved from http://www.royalsociety.org.nz/expert-advice/papers/yr2013/languages-in-aotearoa-new-zealand/

State Services Commission. (2015). *Better public services: Supporting vulnerable children: Result 2: Increase participation in early childhood education*. Retrieved from: http://www.ssc.govt.nz/bps-supporting-vulnerable-children/

Statistics New Zealand. (2006). *QuickStats about culture and identity: Languages spoken: QuickStats about Pacific peoples: Language*. Retrieved from http://www.stats.govt.nz

Statistics New Zealand. (2013). *2013 Census*. Retrieved from http://www.stats.govt.nz/census/

Te Taura Whiri i te Reo Māori. (2015). *About us: Background: Ngā kōrero mua taka mai ki nāianei*. Retrieved from http://www.tetaurawhiri.govt.nz

United Nations. (2008). *United Nations Declaration on the Rights of Indigenous Peoples*. Retrieved from http://www.un.org/esa/socdev/unpfii/documents/DRIPS_en.pdf

Endnotes

1 See http://www.un.org/documents/ga/res/44/a44r025.htm
2 Migrants and/or their descendants from the Pacific Islands now living in Aotearoa New Zealand.

Chapter 2 Language diversity in context: Navigation points

Nola Harvey, Helen Hedges and Valerie N. Podmore

Tē ngaru, tē aha, ka rōnaki te haere (o te waka).
The path of the canoe is smooth when there are no waves
and other obstacles.

Introduction

We acknowledged at the beginning of Chapter 1 that children have a right to their languages, cultures and identities. There are many challenges for children and families where the choice of language for learning is reduced (May & Sleeter, 2010). This study makes a case for broadening the perspectives and possibilities for learning in more than one language, and empowering a fuller and more satisfying and effective participation of diverse families in early childhood education.

This chapter traverses the literature that led to the study, with an emphasis on research undertaken in Aotearoa New Zealand. In addition, we review research about partnerships with families in relation to languages. Partnerships and relationships—and the empowerment that accompanies them—were central to the study. These concepts enabled a sharing of understanding among the research team in order to use them as a basis for considering opportunities and challenges.

The rationale for the study meant that we selected two theoretical framings. These highlight a *credit-based* view of learning in more than one language and the learning resources that accompany languages in families and communities. The final part of this chapter defines key terms we used in the study to ensure all children's languages are viewed positively and result in both linguistically and culturally responsive pedagogies. The chapter concludes with the research questions that guided the study.

Building on previous research about languages

In Aotearoa New Zealand the early childhood Centres of Innovation (COIs) research (2003–2009) included studies of quality practices and innovative teaching in immersion ECE for Māori children, and in a Samoan immersion centre (Meade, 2010). Insights from these studies informed our research. In a kōhanga reo, kaupapa-based action supported children's and whānau members' Māori-language development (Pohatu, Stokes, & Austin, 2006). In addition, at a Māori immersion centre, leadership and whānau development were important for optimal educational experiences and fulfilled lives (Tamati, Hond-Flavell, Korewha, & the whānau of Te Kōpae Piripono, 2008).

Within a Samoan-language immersion context, secure identity and children's learning in their heritage language were important for cognitive learning (Podmore, with Wendt Samu & the A'oga Fa'a Samoa, 2006). The present study built on these findings by exploring the ways languages were *used for learning* rather than the emphasis being on *learning the languages* themselves. After reviewing research and consulting with various groups, Meade, Puhipuhi and Foster-Cohen (2003) identified some key priorities for future Pasifika ECE research. They include: describing children's language experiences, including the range of languages heard in a range of settings; a longitudinal research study on children in immersion (or bilingual) services; and exploring the question "What do parents and communities want?" with regard to pedagogical practices and quality (pp. 41–42). Aspects of these issues and questions are addressed in the present study.

Research at an English-medium kindergarten in partnership with a Samoan immersion centre identified six significant teaching strategies relevant to the children's learning. The core strategy was "teachers help children to revisit their learning experience" to "sustain children's engagement in learning" (Cullen et al., 2009, p. 43). Schofield's (2007) project focused on student teachers' understanding of children's diverse languages. She reported that student-teachers' use of theoretical knowledge of diversity was weak, and that they also identified concerns about their limited knowledge and strategies to support children's uptake of English. However, the bilingual and trilingual student-teachers in the project called upon their prior language learning experiences to develop responsive strategies to link with families and communities. We noted that these two projects were therefore more focused on children's competence in learning concepts in English and/or learning languages rather than language use in learning. Again, this created a space for the present study.

International research on linguistics and bilingualism also adopts a sociocultural approach (Cullen et al., 2009) and emphasises the importance of the home or heritage languages for cognitive learning outcomes (Baker, 2011; Cullen et al., 2009; Podmore et al., 2006). Across the COIs where children were learning in their heritage/home language and/or more than one language, application of sociocultural theoretical concepts (including cultural tools and artefacts) incorporated credit-based perspectives[1]. Nuttall (2010) noted the need for further theory building and critiquing in ECE research projects. Accordingly, our research built on the COI studies by applying the theoretical lenses of cultural and linguistic responsiveness through additive bilingualism (Baker, 2011; Cummins, 2001b, 2009) and funds of knowledge (Gonzalez, Moll, & Amanti, 2005; Moll, Amanti, Neff, & Gonzalez, 1992) to build an understanding of children's learning experiences and outcomes consistent with the aspirations of *Te Whāriki*.

Teacher–family partnerships and learning through languages

Partnership with families or whānau in children's learning is an established feature of the curriculum, philosophy, policy and practice of Aotearoa New Zealand ECE (e.g. Ministry of Education, 1996, 1998, 2002), and, indeed, internationally. Families are not homogeneous, and the four principles of *Te Whāriki* (Ministry of Education, 1996) outlined in Chapter 1—*family and community*, *holistic development*, *relationships* and *empowermen*t—are complex in a diverse society. These complexities are mirrored in the roles of the two partners—families and teachers—in relation to languages, and incorporate consideration of the diversity of family backgrounds, arrangements and types in Aotearoa New Zealand.

As signalled in Chapter 1, we support the position that a first priority in Aotearoa New Zealand is attention to revitalising te reo Māori. This position is consistent with Te One's (2008, p. 68) contention that "Māori children's rights to be educated in Māori" are "an entitlement identified in UNCROC" (i.e. in Article 30 of UNCRC). Te One's study of children's rights in early childhood centres also specifies connections between the right to indigenous language, participation in centre settings, and empowerment of children and their families/whānau.

Studies such as Ritchie and Rau's (2006) have indicated ways in which whanaungatanga (partnerships with families and communities) can be a way to focus attention on te reo and tikanga Māori in early childhood pedagogical practices. Ritchie has led much work on prioritising attention to te reo Māori within both bilingual and English-medium centres (e.g. Ritchie, 2008, 2013). Skerrett and Gunn (2011) also provided evidence in their literature review of the value of sustaining Māori language and culture together to ensure quality experiences in a range of settings.

In relation to education in the heritage/home-language medium, Skerrett and Gunn note that this should be supported for five primary reasons:

- ideologically, because it is an aspect of language rights, which are a component of human rights and a form of protection from discrimination by language
- pedagogically, because it aims to make seamless the progression of children and young people through the education sector without disadvantage
- academically, because it aims to improve academic performance and develop positive attitudes in speakers about their linguistic and cultural identities and heritage/s

- intergenerationally, because it aims to sustain the transmission of language/s, motivated by pride in Pasifika languages, by increasing the public (institutions) and private (homes and communities) domains, which are critical for the survival and maintenance of language/s
- culturally and linguistically, because it aims to uphold diversity in the world (p. 5).

Skerrett and Gunn also highlight the importance of relationships between ECE settings and homes and communities as vital to continuing and valuing bilingual households, and therefore children being able to learn in more than one language.

There is a diversity of expectations and prior experiences across and within families. Studies on quality in parent- and whānau-led services found that Pasifika parents have very high expectations of their ECE centres and teachers: parents wanted both Pasifika languages and cultural maintenance, as well as preparation for successful schooling in English (Mara & Burgess, 2007; Mitchell, Royal-Tangaere, Mara, & Wylie, 2006). These projects suggest that parents and family members, particularly those from indigenous and Pasifika language communities, can feel minimally informed about appropriate provisions for their children who learn in more than one language.

Moreover, families from migrant backgrounds may have moved to Aotearoa New Zealand for work and to fulfil their high aspirations for their children's education. Immigrant and transnational parents may need strong evidence that their children will be successful in a play-based ECE programme (Leaupepe, 2010), and teachers may require deeper understanding of families' aspirations for intergenerational language transfer (McCaffery & McFall-McCaffery, 2010). In this way, teachers might more appropriately meet children's learning needs if they understand parental values and expectations. At the same time, teachers might preserve children's sense of identity as learners, including their linguistic identity as learners who move between different languages and cultures. The present study addressed these concerns by investigating the experiences, priorities and outcomes valued by both parents and teachers. It also enabled teachers to reflect on and analyse their own observations of their language interactions.

A number of authors internationally raise concerns that teachers may adhere unquestioningly to monocultural Western views even when they intend to use inclusive practices. Some literature suggests that there may be a disjuncture in children's experiences between their homes and ECE centres. In Brooker's (2002) study in the United Kingdom, the rich social and cultural capital of Bangladeshi children's family and community environments was not recognised or utilised in the education setting. The all-Anglo teachers were not ignorant of the children's backgrounds, but they believed that creating a play-based learning environment allowed children to learn.

Harvey (2013) explored the narratives of practice of teachers who speak more than one language in the Auckland region. Each used their own languages confidently in the centre and modelled bilingualism as a successful tool for learning, and their stories showed that this usage empowered children and families to bring their heritage/home languages into the centres. One persistent practice that needs addressing in ECE, therefore, is superficial attention to culturally responsive pedagogies (Cowie et al., 2011). This study highlighted the importance of a responsive pedagogical approach to languages and cultures.

A parallel persistent issue that requires attention in teaching practice is therefore attending to languages alongside cultures in demonstrating pedagogical responsiveness. Unless these are linked, tensions can emerge for bi/multilingual families where the cross-generational transfer of languages is a goal (May & Sleeter, 2010; McCaffery & McFall-McCaffery, 2010; Tuafuti, 2010). This has been an issue internationally as well as in Aotearoa New Zealand. Kenner and Ruby (2012) investigated the out-of-school learning of children from multilingual households in the United Kingdom. Their investigation led them to recognise that there are multiple contexts of learning, yet children's multiple identities and their families' communities and heritages were often rendered invisible in formal educational settings.

Evidence from research in Australian prior-to-school educational settings suggests that families of bilingual children can feel silenced and unable to share their aspirations and valued outcomes with teachers. Jones-Diaz (2013) found that parents and children reported diverse experiences in negotiating identities and language retention, and that English came at the expense of other languages in terms of allocation of resources and support. Early childhood teachers in English-medium settings commented that, within a few months of arrival, children who began with little or no English began answering in English and avoided using their heritage/home languages with teachers or parents. Without material resources, institutional and economic support, heritage/home languages and identities suffered (Jones-Diaz, 2013). The "inextricable relationships between culture, language and identity" (Jones-Diaz, 2014, p. 122) highlight the need for teachers who can affirm children's identities and languages as part of critically reflective and socially just practices in ECE services.

If socially just practices are not attended to, "coercive power relations" (Cummins, 2009, p. 261) can arise, where one language and culture is dominant in educational contexts. When this occurs, issues relating to language loss, agency and power can result for children and families who are bi/multilingual and educated in English-medium educational settings. Historical and contemporary challenges associated with the legacy of language loss from one generation to another therefore remain for parents and communities. These challenges are related to loss of control of their children's use of heritage/home languages for learning in environments that favour fluency in English (May, 2008). Tensions arise, then, for bi/multilingual families and children between fostering identities and languages preferred for learning and belonging, and those assigned as the most valuable for achieving success and status in education in Aotearoa New Zealand (May, 2012).

Even well-intentioned and apparently successful collaborations can encounter difficulties. Parents' perspectives on their children's education are often different from what teachers think they are (e.g. Elliott, 2003; O'Gorman & Ailwood, 2012). A small study in Aotearoa New Zealand drew attention to the outcomes related to language and culture valued by Congolese parents with refugee backgrounds whose children participated in mainstream ECE settings (Mitchell & Ouko, 2012). The findings indicated that families had a preference for the employment of teachers who spoke children's heritage/home languages. However, a study of Chinese immigrants in ECE settings showed a disconnection between children's learning experiences at home and in the centre (Guo, 2005, 2012). Chinese parents perceived that serious learning and Chinese cultural experiences occurred at home, whereas the centre was the place where their children learnt English and the practices of the dominant culture. These contrasting findings indicated a need to explore further the ways teachers and families share their ideas about valued outcomes and the ways they engage with each other to learn about and from each other's languages and cultures across a range of settings.

Overall, the literature about partnerships indicates the complexity and wide variation of views that teachers and families hold, and experience, in different ECE settings. To build on current knowledge and inform policy and quality practice, this study provided scope to generate in-depth data on the learning experiences that parents, children and teachers value in ECE centres already making efforts towards partnerships and inclusion. This study therefore potentially opened up conversations among teachers and parents to strengthen shared understanding and stimulate creative, thoughtful and inclusive opportunities, including advocacy for use of heritage/home languages for learning. Such conversations are predicated on the assumption that children's and families' prior knowledge and skills are viewed positively.

Credit-based theoretical perspectives and responses

The images of children that teachers and policy makers have affect the ways teachers view and enact their relationships with families. A persistent issue prevalent in the early childhood literature and underpinning much policy that has a strong influence on teaching practice has been deficit views of children. For example, children who speak more than one language are likely to be viewed as lagging in language development and milestones, which leads to lack of success at initial literacy testing upon arrival at primary school. A cyclical deficit view of Māori and Pasifika children and a continued legacy of an achievement lag persist (McNaughton, 2011; O'Sullivan, Berryman, & Bishop, 2010). Yet recent research on emerging Pasifika bilingual children indicates that, with the appropriate teacher expertise and community support, these children can achieve well (Amituanai-Toloa, McNaughton, Lai, & Airini, 2009; Si'ilata, 2014). This may apply more broadly to children from diverse language and cultural backgrounds if this diversity is similarly viewed positively.

Two theoretical perspectives framed this study. These reflect a credit-based view of children and families who speak more than one language. They provided navigation points for teacher-researchers, in particular, to think about pedagogies and practices that are responsive to languages and cultures. These perspectives were *funds of knowledge* and *additive bilingualism*.

Funds of knowledge

Funds of knowledge is a credit-based notion of everyday knowledge found in families, communities and cultures. Consistent with sociocultural approaches, "the concept of funds of knowledge is based on a simple premise: People are competent, they have knowledge, and their life experiences have given them that knowledge" (González, Moll, & Amanti, 2005, p. ix). A funds of knowledge theoretical lens, applied to children who learn in more than one language, emphasises the need for teachers to extend their understanding of children's diverse learning experiences in their homes, families, communities and cultures (Cooper & Hedges, 2014; Moll, 2000).

The original research in which the term 'funds of knowledge' was coined explored learning and language usage in Mexican–Latino/a bilingual contexts to develop an understanding of human and material resources that could be drawn on for curricular purposes in educational settings (Gonzalez et al., 2005). More recently, teachers and researchers have drawn on the notion of funds of knowledge to develop responsive pedagogies. However, at times researchers may have underplayed linguistic capital, masking the influence of power relations related to policy goals and curricular considerations.

Moll et al. (1992) defined funds of knowledge in bilingual households as the bodies of knowledge, including information, skills and strategies, which underlie household functioning, development and wellbeing. These may incorporate information, ways of thinking and learning, approaches to learning, and practical skills related to more than one language and culture. Examples include economics (such as budgeting, accounting and loans); repair (such as household appliances, fences and cars); and arts (such as music, painting and sculpture) (Moll, 2000).

The notion of funds of knowledge encompasses both the content of young children's early learning and the processes of learning such knowledge through observation and participation in relationships with family members. Researchers have since extended their work to consider wider influences of family and community members, such as siblings, friends and grandparents, including in ECE (Hedges, Cullen, & Jordan, 2011). Kenner (2004) extended the funds of knowledge theoretical approach by regarding families as language and literacy ecosystems. She developed dual language identity texts, building on Cummins's (2001b) additive approach to working in more than one language and Kress's work on multi-literacies. Several publications track the rich development of family and school activities that document the valued experiences of learning in more than one language (Cummins, 2009; Kenner & Kress, 2003).

Funds of knowledge held promise in this study as a way to recognise and embrace children's languages and cultures to the benefit of children. This was because it reduces potential disjuncture in their lives between their homes and educational settings. Moll et al. (1992) have proposed that teachers build on knowledge and practice occurring in children's homes. The concept therefore has the potential for transforming curriculum (see Hensley, 2005). This ensures that educational provision is relevant through drawing on children's experiences and the expertise of families and communities, rather than the educational environment being something far removed from children's understanding.

Additive bilingualism
There is a range of views on the value of bilingualism. Some people may still believe that children will become confused trying to learn in more than one language in an educational setting. In contrast, recent international research has indicated the neural and cognitive values of being bilingual or multilingual (e.g. Barac, Bialystok, Castro, & Sanchez, 2014; Cummins, 2001a). Immersion ECE centres in Aotearoa New Zealand with a goal of bilingualism have a commitment to uphold heritage/home languages, and have pedagogical strategies in place that would benefit from further research. English-medium centres may have some policies of inclusion, but may be wondering how to work appropriately towards promoting, maintaining and/or revitalising a range of heritage/home languages.

An additive bilingual model as a pedagogical approach contends that children can learn effectively in more than one language, and that resources to learn should be provided accordingly (Cummins, 2001a, 2009; Garcia, 2009). An additive model of bilingualism also emphasises the capability of young children to learn effectively in more than one language when this is adequately resourced and supported (Cummins, 2001a, 2001b, 2009; Garcia, 2009). An additive approach occurs in an educational setting where the heritage/home languages, or community or first languages, are acknowledged and not replaced by additional languages. In contrast, subtractive bilingualism occurs where the additional language (e.g. English) replaces the first or heritage/home language.

In contrast, subtractive bilingualism occurs where the additional language (e.g. English) replaces the first or heritage/home language. Subtractive bilingualism is assimilationist and may lead to the loss of the heritage/home language and culture.

Additive bilingualism was first used to guide pedagogy in bilingual education settings, but with the diversity of families increasing it has been applied to English-medium settings where children arrive with diverse language repertoires. We therefore emphasise in this study that we do not see heritage/home languages as additional *per se*; this is the term that was developed as an explanation for appropriate pedagogy. We also see this additive bilingual model as supporting two or more languages.

Genesee (2008) argues that to sustain heritage/home languages children need to be exposed to complex language used in natural and meaningful ways. When children recognise heritage/home languages as meaningful, their agency and empowerment are increased, and stressors are reduced in out-of-home educational settings (Garcia & Wei, 2014).

Definition of terms

In short, children have many linguistic challenges and opportunities that result from participation in different contexts: at home, with peers and teachers at the ECE centre, and in the community with a range of adults and children. The dynamic nature of children's language competence and confidence in different contexts means we need to define terms used in the study carefully. This is also important because of the range of ideologies and perspectives revealed in the literature about the value of learning in more than one language. In our study we use and define terms related to linguistic diversity in the following ways.

- *Heritage/home language:* a contemporary phrase we have selected to use for what may be described elsewhere as mother tongue or L1 or indigenous language. This includes situations where there is family fluency (home) and/or ancestral or cultural identity connections to languages (heritage).
- *Bilingualism:* competence in two languages, but not necessarily similar levels of fluency. Our preferred term would be *emerging bilingualism*, but this term also represents the linguistic competencies of children from households where there may be more than two languages spoken, and thus where there may be a range of associated fluencies. Children who learn in more than one language are also referred to as *emerging bilinguals* in this book.
- *Plurilingualism:* a recent preferred term replacing '*multilingualism*' to describe children's ability to draw on multiple linguistic resources concurrently in two or more languages to achieve effective communication (Garcia & Wei, 2014). The term '*plurilinguals*' to identify those who use more than one language is gaining currency and replacing '*multilinguals*' in educational settings.
- *Transnationals:* families who move countries for work or study. As a result children spend time in different and often contrasting/distinct policy and language contexts for home life and education settings (Garcia & Wei, 2014).
- *Medium of instruction:* the main language used in teaching. The majority of ECE settings in Aotearoa New Zealand do not declare their medium of instruction as English as it is the dominant language for education in Aotearoa New Zealand.
- *Bilingual Education:* There are several models of bilingual education (Baker, 2011). The most effective are full immersion, where 80 percent or more of the instruction time (medium of instruction) is spent in the target language (e.g. ngā kōhanga reo and Pasifika immersion centres in Aotearoa New Zealand), followed by a dual language model, where 50 percent or more of the instruction time is in the target language to be learned and the rest of the time is in English.

- *Māori medium:* a centre where te reo and tikanga Māori are prominent, and teachers use te reo Māori where possible depending on their own proficiency in te reo Māori.
- *English medium:* other ECE centres, usually multi-ethnic, where instruction is in English, te reo Māori is acknowledged to an extent dependent on the teachers' te reo Māori proficiency, and there may be some attempts to incorporate other home languages.
- *Whānau:* a family group, often an extended family group. In contemporary contexts this term may also refer to a kin/community group with a similar philosophy or vision.

As explained in the preface, this study investigates and documents the many ways young children are using their languages for learning; it is not about the learning of languages *per se*.

Research questions and objectives

From this literature review and the associated issues we derived three overarching research questions:

1. What languages do children from participating early childhood education centres use in their learning in the centre and at home?
2. What experiences and outcomes for children who learn in more than one language in the early years are valued by parents, teachers and children?
3. How might the opportunities and challenges for children who learn in more than one language be addressed in educational practice?

The objectives within each of the four different ECE settings were to:

- document the languages spoken by the children, parents and teachers in the ECE centre and at home
- document and interpret the learning experiences of young children who learn in more than one language (as valued by parents, teachers and children)
- document the valued outcomes for young children who learn in more than one language (valued by parents, teachers and children)
- in partnership between teacher-researchers and University of Auckland researchers, analyse and theorise the data gathered, using

funds of knowledge and additive bilingualism approaches, to build on understanding of the learning and teaching of children who learn in more than one language

This chapter has laid out the navigation points—literature, theory and terminology—that guided the study and led to the research questions and objectives. The next chapter describes the study's research design and methods and also presents some quantitative findings.

References

Amituanai-Toloa, M., McNaughton, S., Lai, M. K., & Airini. (2009). *Ua aoina le manogi o le lolo: Pasifika schooling improvement research: Summary report.* Wellington: Ministry of Education.

Baker, C. (2011). *Foundations of bilingualism and bilingual education.* Clevedon, UK: Multilingual Matters.

Barac, R., Bialystok, E., Castro, D., & Sanchez, M. (2014). The cognitive development of young dual language learners: A critical review. *Early Child Research Quarterly, 29*(4), 699–714. doi: 10.1016/j.ecresq.2014.02.003

Brooker, L. (2002). *Starting school: Young children learning cultures.* Buckingham, UK: Open University Press.

Cooper, M., & Hedges, H. (2014). Beyond participation: What we learned from Hunter about collaboration with Pasifika children and families. *Contemporary Issues in Early Childhood, 15*(2), 165–175. doi: 10.2304/ciec.2014.15.2.165

Cowie, B., Otrel-Cass, K., Glynn, T., Kara, H., with Anderson, M., Doyle, J., et al. (2011). *Culturally responsive pedagogy and assessment in primary science classrooms: Whakamana tamariki: Summary report.* Wellington: New Zealand Council for Educational Research.

Cullen, J., Haworth, P., Simmonds, H., Schimanski, L., McGarva, P., & Kennedy, E. (2009). Teacher-researchers promoting cultural learning in an intercultural kindergarten in Aotearoa New Zealand. *Language, Culture and Curriculum, 22*(1), 43–56. doi: 10.1080/07908310802582511

Cummins, J. (2001a). HER Classic Empowering Minority students: Framework for intervention: Author's introduction. *Harvard Educational Review, 71*(4) 649–655.

Cummins, J. (2001b). *Negotiating identities: Education for empowerment in a diverse society* (2nd ed.). Los Angeles, CA: Association for Bilingual Education.

Cummins, J. (2009). Pedagogies of choice: Challenging coercive relations of power in classrooms and communities. *International Journal of Bilingual Education and Bilingualism, 12*(3), 261–271. doi: 10.1080/13670050903003751

Elliott, R. (2003). Sharing care and education: Parents' perspectives. *Australian Journal of Early Childhood, 28*(4), 14–21.

Garcia, O. (2009). *Bilingual education in the 21st century: A global perspective.* Malden, MA: Wiley-Blackwell.

Garcia, O., & Wei, L. (2014). *Translanguaging: Language, bilingualism, and education.* London, UK: Palgrave Macmillan.

Genesee, F. (2008). Early dual language learning. *Zero to Three, 9,* 17–23.

Gonzalez, N., Moll, L. C., & Amanti, C. (Eds.). (2005). *Funds of knowledge: Theorizing practices in households, communities and classrooms.* Mahwah, NJ: Lawrence Erlbaum.

Guo, K. (2005). Asian immigrant parents' and New Zealand early childhood teachers' views of parent–teacher relationships. *New Zealand Research in Early Childhood Education, 8,* 125–134.

Guo, K. (2012). Chinese immigrants in New Zealand early childhood settings: Perspectives and experience. *Early Childhood Folio, 16*(1), 5–9.

Harvey, N. (2013). Principled practices: Respect and reciprocity through linguistically responsive pedagogy. *Early Childhood Folio, 17*(1), 19–23.

Hedges, H., Cullen, J., & Jordan, B. (2011). Early years curriculum: Funds of knowledge as a conceptual framework for children's interests. *Journal of Curriculum Studies, 43*(2), 185–205. doi: 10.1080/00220272.2010.511275

Hensley, M. (2005). Empowering parents of multicultural backgrounds. In N. Gonzalez, L. C. Moll, & C. Amanti (Eds.), *Funds of knowledge: Theorizing practices in households, communities and classrooms* (pp. 143–151). Mahwah, NJ: Lawrence Erlbaum.

Jones-Diaz, C. (2013). Institutional, material and economic constraints in languages education: Unequal provision of linguistic resources in early childhood and primary settings in Australia. *International Journal of Bilingual Education and Bilingualism, 17*(3), 272–286. doi: 10.1080/13670050.2012.754400

Jones-Diaz, C. (2014). Languages and literacies in childhood bilingualism: Building on cultural and linguistic capital in early childhood education. In L. Arthur, J. Ashton, & B. Beecher (Eds.), *Diverse literacies in early childhood: A social justice approach* (pp. 106–125). Camberwell, VIC: Australian Council for Educational Research.

Kenner, C. (2004). *Becoming biliterate: Young children learning different writing systems*. Stoke-on-Trent, UK: Trentham Books.

Kenner, C., & Kress, G. (2003). The multisemiotic resources of biliterate children. *Journal of Early Childhood Literacy, 3*(2), 179–202. doi: 10.1177/14687984030032004

Kenner, C., & Ruby, M. (2012). *Interconnecting worlds: Teacher partnerships for bilingual learning.* London, UK: Institute of Education Press.

Leaupepe, M. T. (2010). Play: A waste of time?: Samoan and Tongan student teachers' views of play. *MAI Review, 1*. Retrieved from http://www.review.mai.ac.nz/index.php/MR/issue/view/15

Mara, D., & Burgess, F. (2007). *O le uluaʻi faitautusi ma le tusitusi: O aʻoaʻoga maoaʻe ma lona aʻoaʻoina I aʻoga amata a le Pasifika: Early literacy: Quality teaching and learning in Pasifika early childhood education.* Wellington: NZCER Press.

May, S. (2008). Language education, pluralism and citizenship. In S. May & H. Hornberger (Eds.), *Encyclopedia of language and education: Vol. 1: Language policy and political issues in education* (pp. 15–29). New York, NY: Springer Science+Business.

May, S. (2012). Contesting metronormativity: Exploring indigenous language dynamism across the urban–rural divide. *Journal of Language, Identity and Education, 13*(4), 229–235. doi: 10.1080/15348458.2014.939036

May, S., & Sleeter, C. (2010). Introduction: Critical multiculturalism: Theory and praxis. In S. May & C. Sleeter (Eds.), *Critical multiculturalism: Theory and praxis* (pp. 1–16). New York, NY: Routledge.

McCaffery, J., & McFall-McCaffery, J. (2010). O tatatou o agaʻi i fea? / ʻOku tatu o ki fe? / Where are we heading?: Pacific languages in Aotearoa New Zealand. *AlterNative Special Supplement Issue Ngaahi Lea ʻa e Kakai Pasifiki: Endangered Pacific Languages and Cultures, 6*(2), 86–121.

McNaughton, S. (2011). *Designing better schools for culturally and linguistically diverse children: A science of performances model for research.* New York, NY: Routledge.

Meade, A. (2010, November). *The contribution of ECE Centres of Innovation to building knowledge about teaching and learning 2003–2010.* Paper presented to TLRI Early Years Symposium, Wellington.

Meade, A., Puhipuhi, H., & Foster-Cohen, S. (2003). *Pasifika early childhood education: Priorities for Pasifika early childhood research: Report to the Ministry of Education.* Wellington: Ministry of Education.

Ministry of Education. (1996). *Te whāriki: He whāriki mātauranga mō ngā mokopuna o Aotearoa: Early childhood curriculum.* Wellington: Learning Media.

Ministry of Education. (1998). *Quality in action: Te mahi whai hua: Implementing the revised statement of desirable objectives and practices in early childhood services.* Wellington: Learning Media.

Ministry of Education. (2002). *Pathways to the future: Ngā huarahi arataki: A 10-year strategic plan for early childhood education.* Wellington: Learning Media.

Mitchell, L., & Ouko, A. (2012). Experiences of Congolese refugee families in New Zealand: Challenges and possibilities for early childhood provision. *Australasian Journal of Early Childhood, 37*(1), 99–107.

Mitchell, L., Royal-Tangaere, A., Mara, D., & Wylie, C. (2006). *Quality in parent/whanau-led services: Summary research report.* Wellington: New Zealand Council for Educational Research / Ministry of Education.

Moll, L. (2000). Inspired by Vygotsky: Ethnographic experiments in education. In C. D. Lee & P. Smagorinsky (Eds.), *Vygotskian perspectives on literacy research: Constructing meaning through collaborative inquiry* (pp. 256–268). Cambridge, UK: Cambridge University Press.

Moll, L., Amanti, C., Neff, D., & Gonzalez, N. (1992). Funds of knowledge for teaching: Using a qualitative approach to connect homes and classrooms. *Theory into Practice, 31*(2), 132–141. doi: 10.1080/00405849209543534

Nuttall, J. (2010, November). *The contribution of the Teaching and Learning Research Initiative to building knowledge about teaching and learning: A review of early years projects, 2004–2010.* Paper presented to TLRI Early Years Symposium, Wellington.

O'Gorman, L., & Ailwood, J. (2012). "They get fed up with playing": Parents' views on play-based learning in the preparatory year. *Contemporary Issues in Early Childhood, 13*(4), 266–275. doi: 10.2304/ciec.2012.13.4.266

O'Sullivan, D., Berryman, M., & Bishop, R. (2010). *Scaling up education reform: Addressing the politics of disparity.* Wellington: NZCER Press.

Podmore, V. N., with Wendt Samu, T., & the A'oaga Fa'a Samoa. (2006). *O le tama ma lana a'oga, o le tama ma lona fa'asinomaga: Nurturing positive identity in children: Final research report from the A'oga Fa'a Samoa, an early childhood Centre of Innovation.* Wellington: Ministry of Education.

Pohatu, H., Stokes, K., & Austin, H. (2006). *Te ohonga ake o te reo: The reawakening of Māori language: An investigation of kaupapa-based actions and change: Te Kohanga Reo o Puau Te Moanaui a Kiwi; Nga Mahi Auaha (Centre of Innovation) 2003–2006.* Wellington: Ministry of Education.

Ritchie, J. (2008). Honouring Māori subjectivities within early childhood education in Aotearoa. *Contemporary Issues in Early Childhood, 9*(3), 202–210. doi: 10.2304/ciec.2008.9.3.202

Ritchie, J. (2013). *Te Whāriki* and the promise of early childhood care and education grounded in a commitment to Te Tiriti o Waitangi. In J. Nuttall (Ed.), *Weaving* Te Whāriki*: Aotearoa New Zealand's early childhood curriculum framework in theory and practice* (2nd ed., pp. 141–156). Wellington: NZCER Press.

Ritchie, J., & Rau, C. (2006). *Whakawhanaungatanga: Partnerships in bicultural development in early childhood care and education: Final report to Teaching and Learning Research Initiative*. Wellington: New Zealand Council for Educational Research.

Schofield, A. (2007). An investigation into the practices of a class of field-based student educators working in linguistically diverse early childhood centres. *Australian Journal of Early Childhood, 32*(2), 23–27.

Si'ilata, R. (2014). Va'a tele: *Pasifika learners riding the success wave on linguistically and culturally responsive pedagogies*. Unpublished doctoral thesis, University of Auckland.

Skerrett, M., & Gunn, A. (2011). *Literature review: Quality in immersion-bilingual early years education for language acquisition: Final report August 2011: Milestone report for Ministry of Education*. Christchurch: University of Canterbury.

Tamati, A., Hond-Flavell, E., Korewha, E., & the whānau of Te Kōpae Piripono, (2008). *Ko koe tēnā kīwai, kau kei tēnei o te kete (You carry your handle and I'll carry my handle): Centre of Innovation report of Te Kōpae Piripono*. New Plymouth: Te Kōpae Piripono, Wellington: Learning Media and Ministry of Education.

Te One, S. J. M. (2008). *Perceptions of children's rights in three early childhood settings*. Unpublished doctoral thesis, Victoria University of Wellington.

Tuafuti, P. (2010). Pasifika additive bilingual education: Unlocking the culture of silence. *MAI Review, 1*. Retrieved from http://www.review.mai.ac.nz/index.php/MR/issue/view/15

Endnotes

1 Credit-based perspectives highlight what children are able to do and are interested in, in contrast with deficit perspectives that tend to highlight what children are as yet unable to do/achieve.

Chapter 3 Researching language diversity: Charting procedures

Peter J. Keegan, Valerie N. Podmore, Nola Harvey and Helen Hedges

Tēnā te ngaru whati, tēnā te ngaru puku.
One wave breaks, another wave swells.

This whakataukī suggests that there are adversities but they can be overcome. It appeared pertinent as our team mapped out and embarked on this collaborative research journey.

Introduction

Languages and literacies are key cultural tools for learning and teaching (Vygotsky, 1978) in early childhood centres, homes and communities. Learners in Aotearoa New Zealand, and in particular young children in the Auckland region, are increasingly likely to speak more than one language (Morton et al., 2014; Statistics NZ, 2006, 2013; see Chapter 1). As reported in Chapter 2, for some time now researchers have reported that there are gaps in our knowledge about children who learn in more than one language, and Meade (2010) has noted the need for ECE centre-wide data. Our research questions, set out in Chapter 2, focused on the languages used and the experiences that are valued for young children who learn in more than one language and that were important for teaching and learning in early childhood education. Cummins (2009) has contended that teachers have an ethical responsibility to understand the role of languages and cultures in children's learning.

Our research approaches acknowledged the richness of language diversity, in keeping with the theoretical framings of funds of knowledge and an additive approach to bilingualism. In short, we did not view language diversity as a problem or a challenge in itself, but viewed children's and families' lived experiences as socially situated in rich, complex communities and worlds. Accordingly, this study collated and reported data that illustrate the diversity of the language experiences of children and their families from four ECE centres in the Auckland region. The primary focus was on children aged from birth to 5 years who participated in ECE centres, their teachers, and their families and whānau.

We have already outlined the policy context, research and theoretical rationale, and the key concepts underpinning the study. From this we developed the three research questions. This chapter describes the research design, which was a mixed-methods study. The chapter also provides quantitative findings across the four ECE settings, including findings from the exploratory use of Observer XT.

Research design

This study used a mixed-method design incorporating questionnaires, focus groups, child interviews and observations across each of the four diverse ECE centre settings. We therefore used a range of quantitative and qualitative methods to address the research questions and to obtain rich data about the valued experiences, outcomes, opportunities and challenges associated with young children learning in more than one language.

This research study was overarched by a "transformative-emancipatory paradigm for mixed-methods research" (Siraj-Blatchford, 2010, p. 202) by applying funds of knowledge and an additive bilingual approach to learning in more than one language. The methodology was primarily inductive, and the research design was collaborative and iterative (Penuel, Fishman, Cheng, & Sabelli, 2011).

The study's methodology was consistent with sociocultural theories that influence *Te Whāriki*, the New Zealand early childhood curriculum (Ministry of Education, 1996). Sociocultural researchers have shown links between language, identity and cultural practices (Rogoff, 2003). The four partner centres comprised a collaborating cluster of ECE centres, so this research was a case study in four settings (Yin, 2014).

Data generation tools and procedures
Our team administered questionnaires to parents and teachers in order to generate data on the languages spoken by children, parents and teachers, and on the valued learning experiences and outcomes for young children who learn in more than one language. We adapted several items from questionnaires that a research programme had used previously to explore te reo Māori use in the home (Keegan, Trinick, & Morehu, 2009). One limitation of this previous survey had been the use of self-report of fluency. It is possible that participants either underestimated or overestimated their fluency in both English and te reo Māori, and this was not corroborated by observational data.

Observations, carried out by the teacher-researchers, included field notes of, and reflections on, children's and parents' arrivals and departures. Thereafter the teacher-researchers' observations in the ECE centres focused mainly on making and reflecting on video clips of children's, teachers', whānau and community members' interactions and the languages used during learning experiences.

Teacher-researchers also recorded video clips of a mat time; that is, a group activity involving teacher/s and children that normally and naturally happened in their centres. We used the mat time video clips to trial the software Human Behaviour Analysis Observer XT 12.5 to analyse excerpts of child–teacher interactions and experiences valued by teachers and parents. Observer XT is a digital coding programme designed to identify and codify the characteristics of different languages used by children in relation to, for example, context and duration, and interaction, personnel and function of language.

Excerpts of video data could therefore be coded in multiple ways. It had proven effective in van Hees's (2011) research on the interactional and discourse patterns of 5- and 6-year-old children in four classrooms when she micro-analysed videos of six case study students and their teachers. Scrutiny of our initial video data had suggested that Observer XT's usefulness, accuracy and consistency would be limited to learning and teaching contexts where a group of children and teachers remained in the same place together, such as in large group contexts or during mat times.

Researchers and teacher-researchers collaboratively held focus group interviews with teachers and parents separately in each centre (i.e. eight focus groups). These occurred in English, Māori or Samoan, as appropriate.

Teacher-researchers also undertook short interviews with older children who were learning in more than one language to discuss their experiences. The focus was on each child's languages and valued learning experiences, and generally took the form of a discussion with the child about her/his portfolio. Teachers' assessments, including narratives, team curriculum documentation and learning stories (Carr & Lee, 2012), supplied further in-depth data on children's learning experiences and outcomes.

Data analyses

The research team used the statistical software package R (R Core Team, 2014) to analyse responses to the questionnaires, entered the data for each item into Microsoft Excel spreadsheets, and computed descriptive statistics. We then generated and presented graphs using the R package ggplot2, via RStudio (RStudio Team, 2014) software to illustrate the questionnaire findings related to research question 1, and transferred the responses to open-ended questions to spreadsheets in order to facilitate further scrutiny and reflection on the data in relation to the research questions.

Within each centre, parent focus group analyses involved searching the transcripts for key themes under each of the three research questions, focusing on the languages used and valued outcomes for children who learn in more than one language. Analyses of the teacher focus group transcripts included searching for key themes related to language/s used, values regarding the learning and teaching of children who learn in more than one language, and effective pedagogical practices. Teacher-researchers worked alongside university researchers to identify the key themes emerging from the focus group interviews, and also selected specific qualitative excerpts that illustrated each of the key themes.

For reporting purposes, transcriptions of the child interviews were translated into English. Teacher-researchers sorted the transcribed child interview data under the research questions, with a particular focus on the child's language use and related valued experiences.

Teacher-researchers selected from the wealth of video data a series of video clips they considered most relevant to the research questions and illustrative of the experiences valued within their centres. The teacher-researchers sorted the transcriptions of these video clips and identified pertinent excerpts that illustrated key points or emergent themes from the research. Transcribers and translators made important contributions to the analyses of these video clips. In addition to the many selected excerpts in te reo Māori or Samoan, at an English-medium centre there were also, for example, excerpts in Japanese and in Mandarin.

Finally, the university researchers trialled the usefulness of Observer XT. This involved analysing short video clips of mat times from each centre.

Participants

Our four participating partner centres represented the languages most prevalent within the Auckland region: English, Māori, Samoan (and Pasifika languages), Hindi and Mandarin. The centres were:

- Te Puna Kōhungahunga, a Māori-medium centre that is a bilingual setting with a goal of Māori as the medium of instruction
- A'oga Fa'a Samoa, a Samoan-immersion centre
- Symonds Street Early Childhood Centre, an English-medium centre with families who speak a wide range of Asian, Middle Eastern and Pasifika languages (children often had parents who spoke more than one heritage/home language, so there were many families where two or three languages were spoken but the language in common between them all was English)
- Mangere Bridge Kindergarten, an English-medium kindergarten with families who speak Pasifika, Asian and European languages.

Ethical considerations

Prior to commencing data generation we obtained ethics committee approvals. We submitted ethics applications to the Human Ethics Committee of the University of Auckland and also to the Auckland Kindergarten Association Research Ethics and Access Committee in relation to Mangere Bridge Kindergarten's participation. Voluntary participation and confidentiality were important considerations. At each centre, parents received an information letter, together with a consent form that included specifying consent for video recording of their child.

The video recordings focused on many aspects of children learning through more than one language. However, measures of the levels of communication were not made, thereby mitigating the possible risk of negative judgements being made about the child or adult participants. The videotapes were not used for assessment or judgements about teacher fluency or competency, or fluency levels of children, but focused on languages used, values embedded in the interactions, what works to sustain interactions, and how language interactions facilitate children's learning. The research team members were also aware that it is "essential to exclude or erase non-consenting persons from the recording or picture" (Podmore, 2006, p. 94). In this book, we simply identify participants as parent, teacher or child in each setting to maintain confidentiality and reduce the risk of identification, wherever possible, given that the names of the centres are known.

Quantitative findings across the partner centres

Ethnic identities and languages spoken

Quantitative analyses across the four centres yielded patterns of data on parents' reported ethnic group identities. There was a range of reported ethnicities at all centres, most notably at Mangere Bridge Kindergarten and Symonds Street Early Childhood Centre. Predictably, at Te Puna Kōhungahunga the majority responded that their ethnicity was Māori, and at the A'oga Fa'a Samoa the prevalent response was Samoan ethnicity. Figure 3.1 shows parents' self-reported ethnic groups(s) as a percentage (of total ethnic group count) for each partner ECE centre.

Figure 3.1: Parents' ethnic groups as a percentage of total ethnic group count for each participating ECE centre

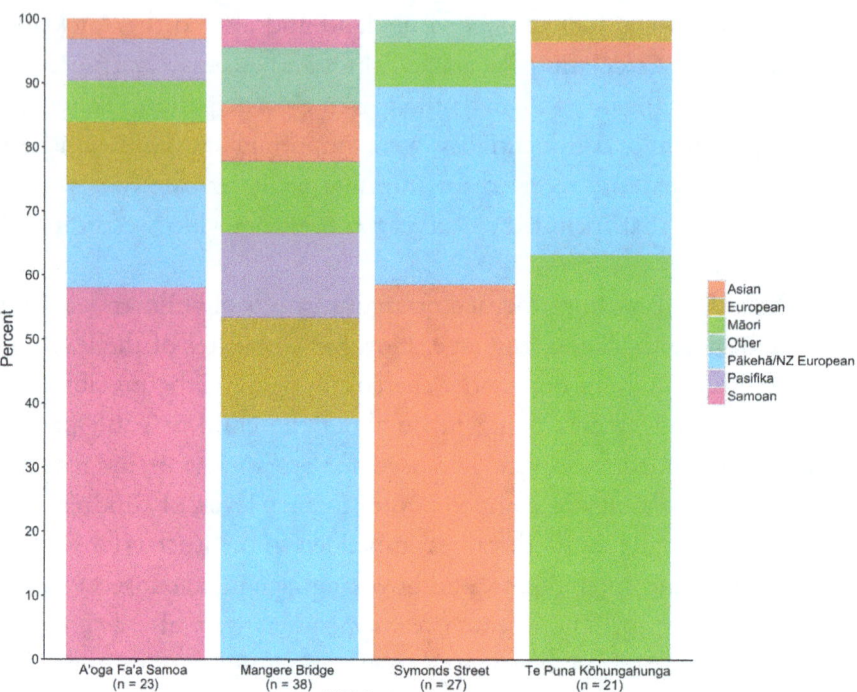

Almost all parents responding to the questionnaires reported that they spoke conversational English. A wide range of spoken languages was evident among parents at Symonds Street Early Childhood Centre and Mangere Bridge Kindergarten.

The number of languages spoken by individual teachers varied across centres (see Figure 3.2, where the teachers are represented using the first letter of the name of the centre). For example, at Symonds Street Early Childhood Centre most teachers spoke several languages and several were fluent in multiple languages, whereas at Mangere Bridge Kindergarten the four permanent teachers were fluent in English only. Kaiako (teachers) at Te Puna Kōhungahunga were almost all fluent speakers of te reo Māori, and faiaoga (teachers) at the A'oga Fa'a Samoa were almost all fluent speakers of Samoan. We were able to code and present individual teachers' multiple languages.

Chapter 3 Researching language diversity: Charting procedures

Figure 3.2: Number of languages spoken by teachers at participating ECE centres

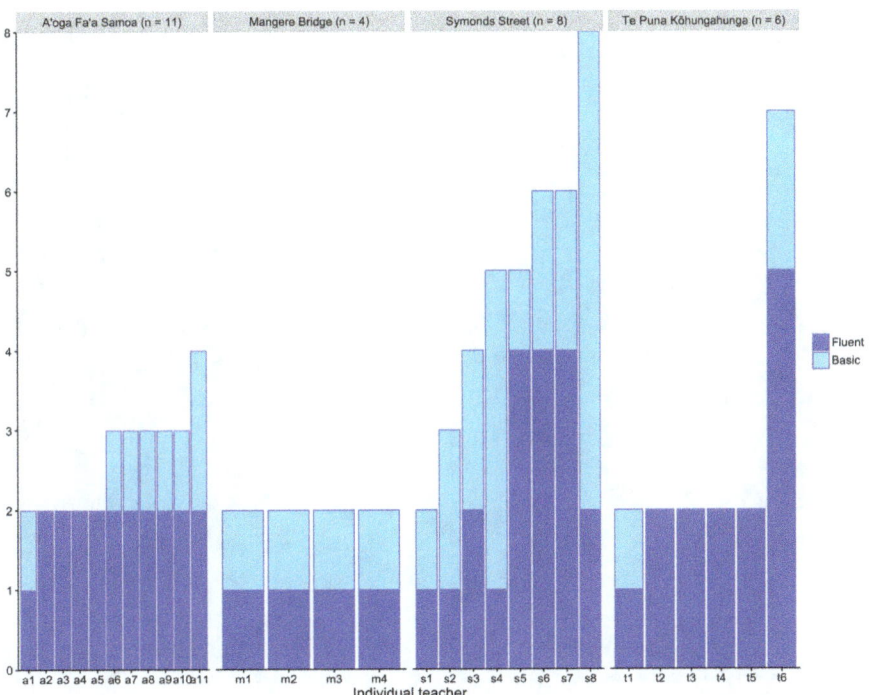

Where possible, we report on te reo Māori proficiency because of the bicultural imperative of *Te Whāriki*. As might be expected, teachers' reported proficiency in te reo Māori was most prevalent at Te Puna Kōhungahunga. However, within all centres almost all teachers reported that they spoke at least simple words and phrases in te reo Māori (Figure 3.3).

Figure 3.3: Proficiency in te reo Māori among teachers at participating ECE centres

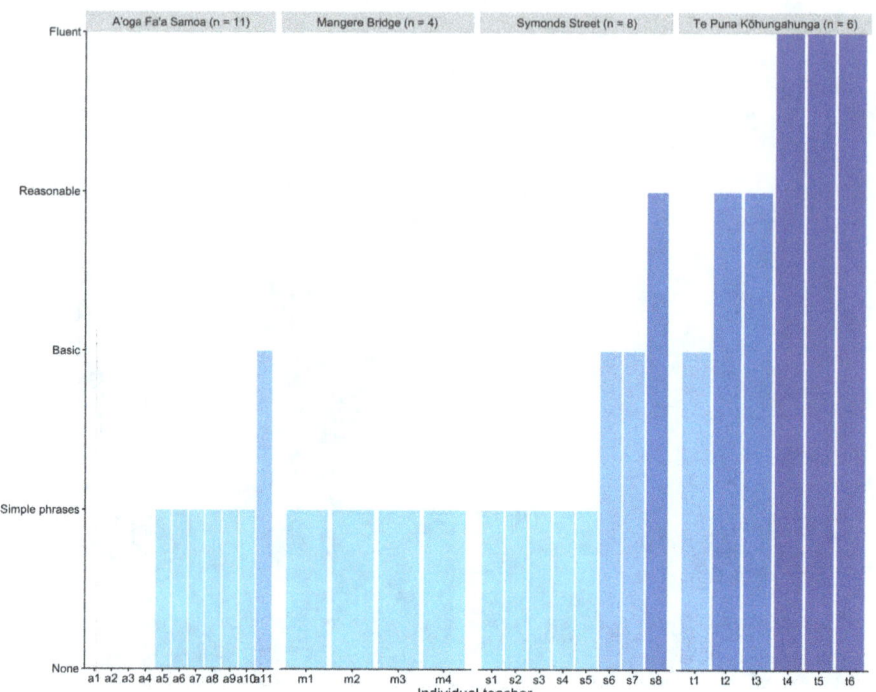

Observer XT analyses

Observer XT proved effective for quantifying and reflecting on patterns of events, behaviours, activities and specific language/s used, as captured by digital video recordings. Our team explored using Observer XT to code spoken language and interaction patterns across similar events recorded at all four partner centres. Teacher-researchers from each centre selected a 3–4-minute video clip of group time or mat time from their video data collection. Each clip was selected as representative of the centre's customary group time activity, and accompanying contextual information and translations were provided.

We coded spoken language use according to the language used, type of language or function of language used, and the speaker(s). Language use is generally mutually exclusive and was readily coded for a particular language (e.g. te reo Māori, Samoan, English, Hindi), or for mixed (and sometimes undetermined) language where one language is being used with vocabulary or phrases from another language.

The speaker may be either an individual (e.g. teacher, parent or child) or a group (such as everybody saying a greeting or singing a song). It was generally straightforward to classify the use of languages that were not the language of instruction in an early childhood centre, as this was often restricted to songs, greetings, instructions and high-frequency words or phrases such as animals, people terms, days of week and colours.

This set of coded analyses focusing on languages yielded information about the languages spoken by the children in the centre (research question 1). We used an Observer XT coding scheme to analyse language across all four partner centres. Not surprisingly, very different patterns of language were used, even when undertaking a similar type of event, such as mat time.

Table 3.1 presents a 200-second snapshot Observer XT analysis of language use during mat times at the ECE centres. Observer XT produces a great deal of numerical and visual displays, which can to be exported to other statistical software or the images used in presentations. The data presented are restricted to the content captured by the video camera, and there were other language exchanges happening simultaneously, especially between children. The durations recorded are unlikely to be perfectly accurate, but they are indicative of the language use observed during events. Accuracy would be improved by having multiple raters examine the same data set.

At the A'oga Fa'a Samoa, the only language used during the observation was Samoan. Seven children greeted their peers and gave their names and background. Five teachers addressed the children. 'All people' was everybody singing a song. The seven durations result from the pauses between the various lines of the song. Te Puna Kōhungahunga observation was almost all in te reo Māori, with one teacher giving instructions in English (to another teacher). Three children stood and gave their pepeha (a saying or motto, often tribally based), with one speaking much longer than the others. All children collectively thanked those who stood. Mangere Bridge's mat time was largely conducted in English, but with greetings in a wide range of languages. Children mostly spoke in English with greetings in various languages. The group collectively sang songs in English and te reo Māori. Symonds Street's mat time was also undertaken mostly in English. The teacher and

Table 3.1: Language use at ECE centres' mat times (200-second duration)

Participant	Language	Total duration (secs)	No.	Participant	Language	Total duration (secs)	No.
A'oga Fa'a Samoa				Te Puna Kōhungahunga			
Child 1	Samoan	1.96	1	Child 1	Māori	49.87	15
Child 2	Samoan	8.79	1	Child 2	Māori	4.12	1
Child 3	Samoan	11.75	1	Child 3	Māori	7.54	3
Child 5	Samoan	15.79	1	All children	Māori	8.46	3
Child 6	Samoan	11.75	1	Teacher A	English	1.42	1
Child 7	Samoan	8.58	1	Teacher B	Māori	0.92	1
Teacher A	Samoan	10.62	1	Teacher C	Māori	68.14	43
Teacher C	Samoan	7.29	4				
Teacher D	Samoan	8.50	1				
Teacher E	Samoan	2.42	1				
All people	Samoan	14.50	7				
Mangere Bridge Kindergarten				Symonds Street ECE			
Child 1	English	1.75	1	Child 1	English	1.12	1
Child 2	Basque	0.67	1	Child 2	English	1.71	1
Child 3	German	0.58	1	Child 3	English	3.75	5
Child 5	English	0.67	1	Child 5	English	13.29	5
Child 6	Irish	0.46	1	Child 6	English	1.29	1
Child 7	English	0.33	1	Child 7	Japanese	6.42	1
Child 8	English	0.96	3	All children	English	6.21	7
Child 9	Chinese	0.54	1	All children	Māori	0.54	1
Child 10	English	1.75	1	All children	Samoan	1.46	1
Teacher A	English	3.50	2	Teacher A	English	93.67	14
Teacher A	English	5.54	3	Teacher A	Chinese	2.58	2
Teacher A	English	1.00	2	Teacher A	Hindi	2.42	2
Teacher A	Vietnamese	0.29	1	Teacher A	Japanese	6.79	3

Teacher A	English	68.04	16	Teacher A	Māori	21.08	9
Teacher B	German	1.12	2	Teacher A	Samoan	1.12	2
Teacher B	Basque	0.08	1	Teacher A	Arabic	1.58	2
Teacher C	Irish	0.25	1	All people	Chinese (Mandarin)	0.67	1
Teacher D	English	120.84	3	All people	Hindi	0.37	1
Teacher D	English	18.83	4	All people	Japanese	1.42	1
Teacher C	English	8.00	3	All people	Māori	10.25	3
All people	Irish	2.50	2	All people	Samoan	0.25	1
All people	English	5.46	3	All people	Arabic	0.46	1
All people	English	15.08	7				
All people	Māori	8.83	2				

children used common greetings in various languages. Most children used English; one child provided Japanese translations of numerals and high-frequency common items. The Māori used was also high-frequency words, including greetings, numerals, people terms, and very common names.

To further explore the capabilities of Observer XT we further coded language exchanges into the coding categories designated for coding types of interchanges and illocutionary forces (i.e. the intentions and effects of interchanges) between child and teacher from the *Inventory of Communicative Acts—Abridged* (INCA-A) scheme proposed by Ninio, Snow, Pan and Rollins (1994). This coding system takes as its observational focus the function of the communicative language, and the verbal and non-verbal interactive behaviours and intentions of speakers and listeners. This proved to be a relatively straightforward, if very time-consuming, process. We could not always agree on our interchange classifications and would require expert input before we could confidently report results, but it did demonstrate the capabilities of the Observer XT software.

A short example of the many types of codes that may be used is presented in Table 3.2.

Table 3.2: Example of codes that can be used for Observer XT classification of data

Teacher or child interchange type codes (visuals or actions)	Eliciting code	Clarification code
DJF: discuss joint focus	AC: answers call to	CL: Call attention to hearer by name
NIA: negotiate into activities or roles		
NMA: establish mutual attentiveness		
PRO: perform moves /activities or parts of games		
MRK: marking (this includes praise)		

Observer XT allows for the classification of interaction types, frequency and durations. It also allows comparison of interaction types between participants (such as teachers and children). Interaction types can be compared within both similar partner centre activities and across the four partner centres. Interactions can also be classified and analysed by language use.

Our research team identified both strengths and limitations associated with the use of Observer XT in ECE settings. Observer XT has extremely powerful analytical capabilities, but the analytical processes require intensive skill learning. It works best with videos that effectively capture all speaker activities. This is not straightforward in ECE settings, where children are often moving around. Coding of interactions and language use can then be very laborious and time consuming. In this study the visual coverage of all children interacting with their teacher/teachers was constrained by the use of a single camera, but audio tracking was possible for all talk and exchanges. Restricting the use of Observer XT to mat times would be considered a limitation within early childhood settings. Overall, however, within these specific constraints, Observer XT was useful for quantifying observations, reflecting on patterns, coding interactions, and determining the duration of interactions in the target languages.

Summary

This chapter has presented an overview of the research design and methodology developed for this mixed-methods study of children who learn in more than one language. Quantitative findings from questionnaires in four diverse early childhood settings provided useful information about both the ethnicities of and languages spoken by teachers and parents. The research team coded and analysed video observations of mat time to explore the use of Observer XT in early childhood settings. These results were introduced and the usefulness of Observer XT as a tool was appraised as having specific strengths and weaknesses. The next four chapters—one from each of the four partner ECE centres—describe the centres and their philosophies, and present primarily qualitative findings from within each setting.

References

Carr, M., & Lee, W. (2012). Learning stories: Constructing learner identities in early education. Los Angeles, CA: Sage.

Cummins, J. (2009). Pedagogies of choice: Challenging coercive relations of power in classrooms and communities. *International Journal of Bilingual Education and Bilingualism, 12*(30), 261–271. doi: 10.1080/13670050903003751

Keegan, P. J., Trinick, A. B., & Morehu, T. R. O. (2009). *He kāinga kōrerorero: Project one— baseline survey, final report prepared for Te Puni Kōkiri: He kāinga kōrerorero: Project one— baseline survey*. Auckland: UniServices.

Meade, A. (2010, November). *The contribution of ECE Centres of Innovation to building knowledge about teaching and learning 2003-2010*. Paper presented to TLRI Early Years Symposium, Wellington. Retrieved from http://www.tlri.org.nz

Ministry of Education (1996). *Te whāriki: He whāriki mātauranga mō ngā mokopuna o Aotearoa: Early childhood curriculum*. Wellington: Learning Media. Retrieved from http://www.education.govt.nz/early-childhood/teaching-and-learning/ece-curriculum/

Morton, S. M. B., Atatoa Carr, P. E., Grant, C. C., Berry, S. D., Bandara, D. K., Mohal, J., et al. (2014). *Growing up in New Zealand: A longitudinal study of New Zealand children and their families: Now we are two: Describing our first 1000 days*. Auckland: Growing Up in New Zealand.

Ninio, A., Snow, C. E., Pan, B., & Rollins, P. (1994). Classifying communicative acts in children's interactions. *Journal of Communication Disorders, 27*, 157–188. doi: 10.1016/0021-9924(94)90039-6

Penuel, W. R., Fishman, B. J., Cheng, B. H., & Sabelli, N. (2011). Organising research and development at the intersection of learning, implementation, and design. *Educational Researcher, 40*(7), 331–337. doi: 10.3102/0013189X11421826

Podmore, V. N. (2006). *Observation: Origins and approaches to early childhood research and practice.* Wellington: NZCER Press.

R Core Team. (2014). *R: A language and environment for statistical computing* [software]. Retrieved from http://www.R-project.org/

Rogoff, B. (2003). *The cultural nature of human development.* New York, NY: Oxford University Press.

RStudio Team. (2014). *RStudio: Integrated development for R* [software]. Retrieved from http://www.rstudio.com/

Siraj-Blatchford, I. (2010). Mixed-method designs. In G. MacNaughton, S. A. Rolfe, & I. Siraj-Blatchford (Eds.), *Doing educational research: International perspectives on theory and practice* (pp. 193–208). Crows Nest, NSW: Allen & Unwin.

Statistics New Zealand. (2006). *QuickStats about culture and identity: Languages spoken: QuickStats about Pacific peoples: Language.* Retrieved from http://www.stats.govt.nz

Statistics New Zealand. (2013). *2013 Census.* Retrieved from http://www.stats.govt.nz/census/

van Hees, J. (2011). *Oral expression of five and six year olds in low socio-economic schools.* Unpublished EdD thesis, University of Auckland.

Vygotsky, L. S. (1978) *Mind in society: The development of higher mental processes.* Cambridge, MA: Harvard University Press.

Yin, R. K. (2014). *Case study research: Design and methods* (5th ed.). Applied Social Research Methods Series (Vol. 5). Thousand Oaks, CA: Sage.

Chapter 4 Te Puna Kōhungahunga

Jasmine Castle, Marama Young, Karen Liley, Peter J. Keegan and Tania Popata

Ko te manu e kai ana i te miro, nōna te ngahere.
Ko te manu e kai ana i te mātauranga, nōna te ao.
The bird who feeds from the miro owns the forest.
The bird who feeds off knowledge claims the world.

Introduction

Te Puna Kōhungahunga is a Māori-medium ECE centre based at the Epsom campus (the former Auckland College of Education) of the University of Auckland. It is a mixed-age centre, with 53 tamariki enrolled at the time of data collection, and eight permanent, full-time kaiako (teaching staff). The centre's philosophy of whanaungatanga (kinship/whānau-type relationships and inclusivity) is linked directly to the above whakataukī (proverb). The kaupapa (vision/philosophy) is whānau driven to enable tamariki mokopuna (younger children) to be confident, capable and competent ki te taha Māori me te taha Pākehā (bilingual and bicultural learners). Kaiako describe the centre curriculum as diverse, practical and ultimately holistic in the sense that the many regular activities include: hīkoi maunga (walk to and on mountain), swimming, hosting and attending pōwhiri (traditional Māori welcomes), and attending annual noho marae (marae visits).

Te Puna Kōhungahunga leadership and management have been consistent and strong for the past decade, with a centre manager who has built extensive relationships in Auckland, Aotearoa New Zealand and abroad. These relationships are not restricted to ECE: they extend across many communities and disciplines and are nurtured continuously, with many of the centre whānau remaining involved directly or indirectly with the centre.

Research participants

Six teaching staff at Te Puna Kōhungahunga completed questionnaires and participated in the kaiako focus group. Five whānau (parents) participated in the whānau focus group, representing four tamariki (both parents of one child participated). Of the people present at the whānau focus group, past whānau were represented by both the facilitator and the recorder. As an icebreaker for the participating whānau, the facilitator and recorder spoke about their own children's experiences at Te Puna Kōhungahunga and how these influenced their own journeys with te reo Māori.

In addition to compiling their usual learning story portfolios, kaiako chose 20 tamariki, selected to balance gender, languages and ethnic groups. Together, kaiako and individual tamaiti (children) revisited photographs about their learning experiences and situations, thereby eliciting further kōrero (discussion) about learning. This process provided one-to-one time with tamariki, with opportunities to build confidence and trust among several less vocal, less confident children.

Languages spoken by the children in the centre and at home

Research question 1: What languages do children from participating ECE centres use in their learning in the centre and at home?

All kaiako spoke te reo Māori, albeit with varying degrees of fluency. Teacher (kaiako) questionnaire data showed that three were fluent (one was a native speaker), two reported a reasonable level of fluency, and one had a basic knowledge. In addition to te reo Māori and English, there were kaiako (including regular relievers) who were able to speak one or more other languages, and these languages included: New Zealand Sign Language, German, French, Spanish and Japanese. Kaiako questionnaire findings and their focus group dialogue consistently advocated that tamariki should learn through te reo Māori me ōna tikanga (Māori language and associated cultural practices), and experience consistency in daily routines and practices.

Figure 4.1: Te Puna Kōhungahunga kaiako and parents' te reo Māori proficiency as a percentage

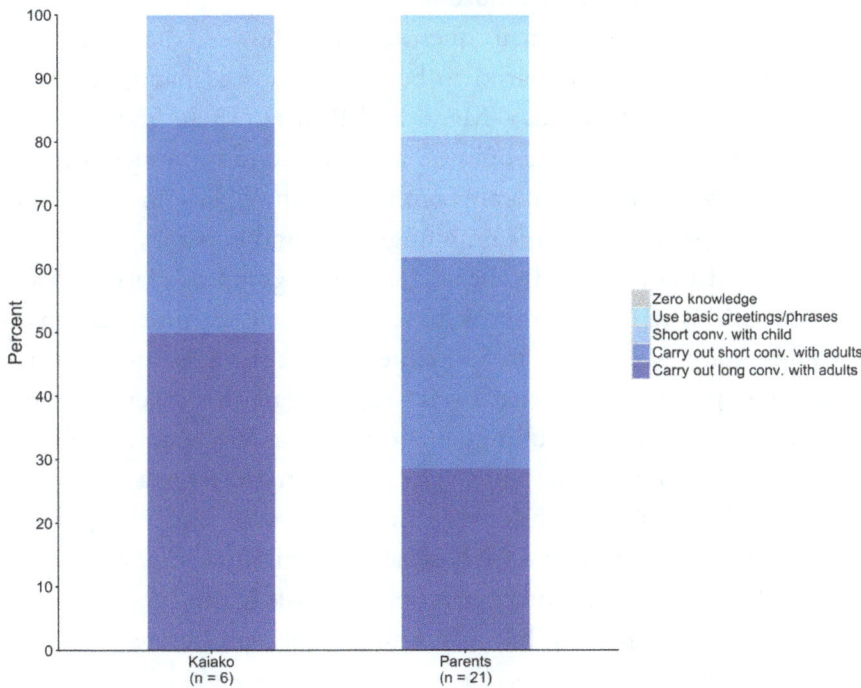

Kaiako and parents' (whānau) te reo Māori proficiency are presented as percentages in Figure 4.1. Among parent (whānau) questionnaire respondents, all reported at least basic proficiency in te reo Māori, 80 percent could carry out short conversations with their child, around 60 percent could carry out short conversations with adults, and almost 30 percent could carry out long conversations with adults.

The teacher-researchers reported that the questionnaire data were valuable for assessing the languages spoken by whānau. For example, the kaiako learnt that Spanish or French were third languages for three whānau. They were able to choose one trilingual whānau (German, English and Māori) to be part of the whānau focus group discussion, as well as three other whānau strongly committed to Te Puna Kōhungahunga kaupapa.

Valued experiences and outcomes for tamariki (children)

Research question 2: What experiences and outcomes for children who learn in more than one language in the early years are valued by parents, teachers and children?

Findings from the whānau questionnaire showed that generally whānau wanted their tamariki to be competent and happy to stand confidently in both worlds—Māori and Pākehā. These findings link directly to the centre philosophy at Te Puna Kōhungahunga of capable, competent learners who are confident in their place in the world. There was a strong emphasis on bilingualism and biliteracy, as well as overall academic success. In the whānau focus group one father stated he wanted his children to speak te reo Māori all the time. This parent's passion for bilingualism and biliteracy was strongly voiced in the focus group discussion: "what I want for him [and his other children] is … I want them to be bilingual and biliterate Māori and English". Te Puna Kōhungahunga philosophy demonstrates taonga tuku iho, the holistic transfer of knowledge and spirituality. This is a passion which was passed down from his father and will now be passed down to his children, and this intergenerational knowledge and commitment are special to witness. While not a full immersion centre, Te Puna Kōhungahunga offers the space to provide enough te reo Māori to cater for a range of learners and backgrounds.

Key themes were established across the questionnaire and focus group data. The themes were derived from the philosophy of Te Puna Kōhungahunga, with links to four tools that are used in the centre's daily curriculum, assessment and planning processes: *Te Whāriki* and *Te Whatu Pōkeka* (Ministry of Education, 1996, 2009); *Te Hāpai Ō* (Jenkins, Harris, Morehu, Sinclair, & Williams, 2012); and *Tātaiako* (Ministry of Education & New Zealand Teachers Council, 2011).

The kaiako reported that the key themes cannot be explained separately because they are closely interconnected, and there were often multiple āhuatanga (appearances/circumstances) for each whānau response. These six key themes are interlinked and mesh together: whanaungatanga (relationships); kaitiakitanga (guardianship); manaakitanga (to support, take care of); wairuatanga (spirituality); tangata whenuatanga (indigeneity, belongingness); and tuakana/teina (mentorship). Data from kaiako and whānau questionnaires and focus groups, together with video recordings, support these interwoven themes.

Questionnaire responses showed that whanaungatanga was important, and that relationships and connections to te ao Māori (the Māori world) were both tangible and intangible. As a whānau member explained:

> I came here just because of the way they do things … the whanaungatanga the way that the Puna [Te Puna Kōhungahunga] is driven by the whānau … All of the kaiako and the staff they're all like, well, 'We're a staff member here but at the end of the day whatever you want then that's what we'll do.' So even that philosophy is a very Māori philosophy, that you give it back to the whānau to, you know, kei a rātou te mana whakahaere [they—the whanau—have input into decision making]. (Parent 1, whānau focus group).

The diversity of whānau cultures at Te Puna Kōhungahunga was evident. Kaiako and whānau responses indicated that with whanaungatanga connections children could become confident to achieve their aspirations. As one kaiako explained:

> I assume by bringing their children to Te Puna Kōhungahunga they support our values of whanaungatanga, manaakitanga, biculturalism, te ao Māori, but by having a kōrero with parents, I learn about their hopes and values. (Kaiako 1, kaiako focus group)

All focus group whānau had children who started at Te Puna Kōhungahunga as babies and they were there for the relationships fostered. One parent stated that coming to Te Puna Kōhungahunga was not for te reo Māori exclusively, but for the whanaungatanga and the whānau-driven kaupapa. Another whānau grew up on the marae, but because they found it difficult to provide this experience within an urban setting, whanaungatanga and manaakitanga fostered at Te Puna Kōhungahunga were important for the tamariki and whānau.

Kaiako described how whanaungatanga gave the whānau confidence to belong and to be responsive and proactive to look after others—*manaakitanga*. Questionnaire and focus group responses from whānau emphasised that bilingual and biliterate aspects and overall academic achievement were important to whānau. Some parents want bilingualism, but also suggested that multilingualism is important:

> We will support our child's trilingualism as best we can. We also hope she will learn more languages at school. We'd like her to confidently participate in both the Pākehā and Māori worlds thereby showing those around her that having more than one language enriches your life and doesn't hinder your development. (Parent 19, questionnaire)

> We want her to have a grounded sense of self and her Māori identity, tikanga and reo. And that [she] learns in te reo and in English. (Parent 9, questionnaire)

> Comfortable in the ao Māori and Pākehā. Be able to travel, explore the world and other cultures, be multilingual. (Parent 16, questionnaire)

> Ako i ngā reo e rua. Ka whakapiki ōna wheakotanga, kei roto, kei waho hoki i te akomanga. [Learn in two languages, wide variety of learning experiences both inside and outside of the classroom.] (Parent 17, questionnaire)

> I would like my child to be able to code switch between Māori and English easily and fluently. I would also like him to explore all parts of his reo through creativity. (Parent 2, questionnaire)

The focus group whānau indicated that their tamariki and mokopuna are the ones who will carry on te reo Māori and tikanga (Māori practices and principles):

> I want for them to graduate high school to be at the same level, be super confident in both worlds and not just language not just in terms of the language, … where they're from, you know, all of that to be [a] strong base as well. (Parent 1, whānau focus group)

> For [daughter] just to have confidence in herself and everything that she does to be bilingual. (Parent 2, whānau focus group)

> Same as (other parent) I want her to be a confident bilingual speaker. (Parent 3, whānau focus group).

In regard to *wairuatanga*, kaiako commented on spiritual connections to the land. Video recordings on the whāriki (mat times) showed tamariki confidently participating in karakia and waiata (prayers and songs). In the focus groups, kaiako and whānau emphasised how *manaakitanga* is embedded in the philosophy of being Māori. One whānau spoke about commitment to the kaupapa of Te Puna Kōhungahunga, and stated that commitment was across all aspects of whānau life.

> Ki a au he maumau te reo, kāore i te mau ki te manaakitanga me ērā atu kaupapa Māori. [To me, te reo Māori has no real purpose unless it's tied to other Māori values and practices such as manaakitanga.] (Kaiako 3, kaiako focus group)

> Being respectful to others (manaakitanga). Creative. (Parent 12, questionnaire)

The theme of *tangata whenuatanga* was woven through the comments of both kaiako and whānau. All kaiako responding to the questionnaire stated that pepeha, karakia, waiata, Maungawhau (the nearby mountain; i.e. Mount Eden), pōwhiri, and noho marae were focal parts of everyday Te Puna Kōhungahunga life. Three of the whānau at the focus group reported their commitment to supporting (by coming to help) on noho marae and visits up Maungawhau.

Questionnaire responses from some whānau showed they wanted their tamariki to help others; to be socially confident and competent not only in Te Puna Kōhungahunga but also in the bush, the community and the home; and to have equal opportunity. Aspirations for children included:

> Confident, independent learner who engages positively with other tamariki, to be able to waiata and kōrero Māori, to understand

tikanga and protocols. To have a strong foundation and values to navigate in a bilingual world. (Parent 19, questionnaire)

Whanaungatanga, tikanga Māori, to be creative and confident in everything she does. (Parent 6, questionnaire)

Help others especially in terms of advancing the needs and aspirations of Māori. (Parent 14, questionnaire)

Kaiako stated in the questionnaires that *tuakana/teina*—older tamariki looking after younger ones—occurs naturally, even among the babies. They gave examples of the contexts where this was evident: pānui pukapuka (reading), wā whāriki (mat time), hīkoi Maungawhau (group walking up and on Maungawhau), and play.

Opportunities and challenges

Research question 3: How might the opportunities and challenges for children who learn in more than one language be addressed in educational practice?

Kaiako considered that a positive outcome of these multiple themes was that they had come to realise that these āhuatanga (circumstances) are always interconnected in all aspects of Te Puna Kōhungahunga practices and approaches.

> As an example we will use our fortnightly Maungawhau hīkoi to illustrate all themes. Our centre philosophy is based on whanaungatanga and our hīkoi aren't possible without whānau to support our teacher ratios. Our whānau are able to get to know each other during these hīkoi. One of our whānau lives on the maunga as kaitiaki [guardian] and he shared valuable insights and knowledge about the maunga and local tikanga [tangata whenuatanga]. [This was evident in the video data of interactions.] Our relationship with Maungawhau allows us to naturally practise wairuatanga and our spiritual connection not just to the land but to the language we use. One of our kaiako composed a karakia that we use to teach acknowledgement, respect, and gratitude for tūpuna and iwi. Tuakana/teina relationships are present between kaiako/whānau and tamariki as well as amongst themselves (especially our new 2-year-olds coming up for the first time). This aspect flows on to the āhuatanga of manaakitanga where everyone is responsible for self-care, care for each other, as well as their wider environment. (Kaiako 1 and Kaiako 2)

An important result of the research data findings is that Maungawhau and whāriki practices have been the subjects of ongoing self-reviews for the past 2 years at Te Puna Kōhungahunga. Te Puna Kōhungahunga have been visiting Maungawhau since 2012 and it has been noted that in the span of 3 years the kaiako, whānau and tamariki have grown in confidence and appreciation of the physical, spiritual and interpersonal aspects of these hīkoi. The idea of taking pre-schoolers on the maunga—rain or shine—was a challenge for kaiako and whānau alike, but nature and the environment is such a vital space for some tamariki who like to be outdoors. Added to this is the wairuatanga connection with Maungawhau and the sense of belonging here, in this space.

The commitment to the ongoing improvement of practice at Te Puna Kōhungahunga is also reflected in self-review subjects, which include "What is your commitment to te reo Māori, how do you use te reo Māori in your daily life and how are you building on your knowledge?" and "What is your personal philosophy and how does it align to Te Puna Kōhungahunga philosophy?" These questions are addressed to both kaiako and whānau alike in an effort to maintain and strengthen commitment to the overarching kaupapa of Te Puna Kōhungahunga.

While there are a number of different teaching philosophies in any one centre, within this Māori-medium setting the whānau and staff have committed specific times throughout the day to actively practise tikanga Māori using te reo Māori as the primary language. Karakia and mihimihi at morning and afternoon mat times provide opportunities for whānau and tamariki to learn, participate in and experience tikanga in a formal setting. While the time-frame is a maximum of 15 minutes, this daily immersion is essential so that the intended purposes and goals can be fostered. The session includes waiata, hīmene (hymns), mihimihi, and pepeha. It is a space that can create and foster a sense of belonging and that allows everyone to acknowledge one another, and people's atua and their tribal or non-tribal connections.

One challenge relating to the morning wā whāriki and pepeha, in particular, was how to support whānau who had migrated to Aotearoa New Zealand and their children who were born here. How can one create a sense of belonging or tangata whenuatanga (belongingness/indigeneity) for whānau who are in this position? How can one incorporate a child's whakapapa (genealogy) and support their identities and connections to Aotearoa New Zealand? After some initial conversations between the kaiako, the self-review will be an ongoing process with in-depth research and conversations between whānau, parents, staff, the wider community, kaumātua (male elders) and kuia (female elders).

One aspect of the review will be looking into what constitutes identity and what it means for Te Puna Kōhungahunga whānau. The review will be discussed as a whānau, but it will also be an individual journey for each whānau. The review process may be the first time whānau have been asked to reflect upon their 'identity', not just for pepeha purposes but also to think about their connections to people, places and the history of those relationships. This can be a daunting process for some, but from past experience the journey outcomes have been positive and engaging. Initially the pepeha rests with the parents, but as the child grows and makes connections of their own, their pepeha may change to suit them.

In this scenario an opportunity arises for Te Puna Kōhungahunga to consider changing the oral format of how the pepeha is presented. The current format for pepeha consists of maunga, awa, moana, waka, marae, iwi and ingoa (mountain, river, sea, canoe, marae, tribe and name). With whānau in mind who have no Māori connection to landmarks or pepeha, kaiako now encourage whānau to think of connections they could use for their pepeha, which are normally slotted into the generic pepeha format. The purpose is inclusion and giving the whānau a sense of belonging, but it is here the opportunity arises to add or tailor the pepeha to suit the child. For example, additions may include "Ko ... toku māmā." "Nō ... ia" (" ... is my mother. She is from ..."). Instead of "Ko Ngāti Whātua te iwi" ("Ngāti Whātua is my iwi"), the sentence "Kei Mt Albert tōku kāinga" ("My home is at Mt Albert") could be used. A personalised change to the format may be slightly easier for whānau and could potentially create a te reo Māori extension for older tamariki who currently have pepeha.

Over the course of the research project wā whāriki has undergone a number of changes as a result of new kaiako and their teaching philosophies, children leaving, the increase in the number of babies, and closer observations from the video data recorded for the project. Data collected from the whānau focus group showed that most whānau want their children to know their pepeha and feel confident to stand and deliver it.

The observation that standing to present one's pepeha outside of the centre can be intimidating and challenging for the child led to slight changes being made to the process of wā whāriki. Pepeha were previously presented by the child, who stood where they were on the mat and were assisted by the kaiako. This later changed to the child standing next to the kaiako in front of the rōpū (group). The reasoning behind the change was so that kaiako are right by their side to assist the child physically with a reassuring hand and with a quieter tone to cue or lead their pepeha. The kaiako are also in a better position to scan the whāriki consistently and to manage and communicate with the others. At present a mixture of the two processes is practised, which normally depends on the leading kaiako. While all the kaiako have their own philosophies regarding wā whāriki, we realise the importance of adapting our own practices to accommodate the daily sessions, thereby acknowledging that each day is a new day with new scenarios.

Conclusion

During the process of the research at Te Puna Kōhungahunga, kaiako became more conscious of the whānau aspirations for their tamariki and how these affect centre practice. The data collected enabled deeper kaiako relationships with tamariki, whānau and one another. Kaiako put strategies in place to encourage more meaningful one-on-one tamaiti interactions, to improve assessment and planning methods and ultimately provide valuable learning experiences and outcomes for tamariki. The kaiako came to know more about the parents and children through administering the parent questionnaire and through the process of the whānau focus group. For example, teachers learnt more about the languages spoken in the children's homes, and about parents' aspirations for their tamariki. A teacher-researcher explained further that "we now know the whānau have languages other than te reo Māori, but they want their children to [prioritise] te reo Māori and to be bilingual and biliterate".

Through child interviews and discussions with young children about the learning stories and portfolios, teachers listened in greater depth to individual children. As a result of the research, these types of in-depth discussions about each child's portfolio, languages and whānau aspirations for children became more systematic and established practices at the centre. Te Puna Kōhungahunga have moved increasingly towards full immersion, and although respecting diversity, there is a commitment to becoming a full immersion centre. This movement towards full immersion in te reo Māori was supported by the research, but was also due to dynamic changes in enrolments, with more babies starting at the centre towards the end of the research project.

References

Jenkins, K., Harris, P., Morehu, C., Sinclair, E., & Williams, M. (2012). *Te hāpai ō: Induction and mentoring in Māori-medium settings.* Wellington: New Zealand Teachers Council. Retrieved from http://www.teacherscouncil.govt.nz/content/te-hapai-o

Ministry of Education. (1996). *Te whāriki: He whāriki mātauranga mō ngā mokopuna o Aotearoa: Early childhood curriculum.* Wellington: Learning Media.

Ministry of Education. (2009). *Te whatu pōkeka: Kaupapa Māori assessment for learning early childhood exemplars.* Wellington: New Zealand: Learning Media. Retrieved from http://www.educate.ece.govt.nz/learning/curriculumAndLearning/Assessmentforlearning.aspx

Ministry of Education & New Zealand Teachers Council. (2011). *Tātaiako: Cultural competencies for teachers of Māori learners.* Wellington: Author. Retrieved from http://www.minedu.govt.nz/TheMinistry/EducationInitiatives/Tataiako

Chapter 5 The A'oga Fa'a Samoa: A Samoan-immersion centre

Eneleata Tapusoa, Valerie N. Podmore, Patisepa Tuafuti, Jan Taouma and May Crichton

O le tama ma lana a'oga,
o le tama ma lona fa'asinomaga.
(Nurturing positive identity in children.)

Introduction

The A'oga Fa'a Samoa is a Samoan-language immersion centre located in the grounds of Richmond Road Primary School in Ponsonby, Auckland. The centre began operating in 1984, and in 1990 it became the first licensed and chartered Pacific Island centre in Aotearoa New Zealand (Taouma, Tapusoa, & Podmore, 2013). The centre is staffed by 12 registered teachers. It is licensed for 50 children, and up to 16 of them can be aged under 2 years.

The A'oga Fa'a Samoa has developed a philosophy statement supported by research on language immersion and bilingualism. This statement shows evidence of connections between children's learning of their heritage/home language, their identity and their educational success (Cummins, 2001a, 2001b, 2009; Tuafuti, 2010; Tuafuti & McCaffery, 2005). The philosophy states that the A'oga Fa'a Samoa will:

- promote Samoan language and culture, so nurturing the positive identity of the children
- employ trained educators and encourage further training so that quality care and education are provided
- encourage a family atmosphere for parents and children so children feel secure and loved
- emphasise enjoyment of learning through the medium of the Samoan language.

Consistent with the centre's philosophy, teachers use the Samoan language to deliver the curriculum and the holistic learning programme. Teachers speak Samoan only, documentation is in Samoan, and books and teaching resources are written in Samoan. Teachers encourage the children's parents to attend Samoan language classes in the community. English-speaking areas are set up in the centre for visitors, parents and family members who are not fluent Samoan speakers.

Overarching values

Prior to participating in the present project, the A'oga Fa'a Samoa had been selected as an early childhood Centre of Innovation (COI). Pasifika values influenced both the centre of innovation research that took place between 2003 and 2006, and the TLRI research that we carried out between 2013 and 2015. Samu (as cited in Podmore, with Wendt Samu, 2006) contended that the success of Pasifika research is dependent on whether the design and processes are informed by Pasifika values. Accordingly, the values that underpinned the research at the A'oga Fa'a Samoa included: *alofa* (love and commitment), *tautua* (service and responsibility) and *fa'aaloalo* (respect) (Podmore, with Wendt Samu, 2006, p. 38). The values are illustrated in this *poutu* model (Figure 5.1):

Figure 5.1: The *poutu* model, showing the three values that informed our research at the A'oga Fa'a Samoa

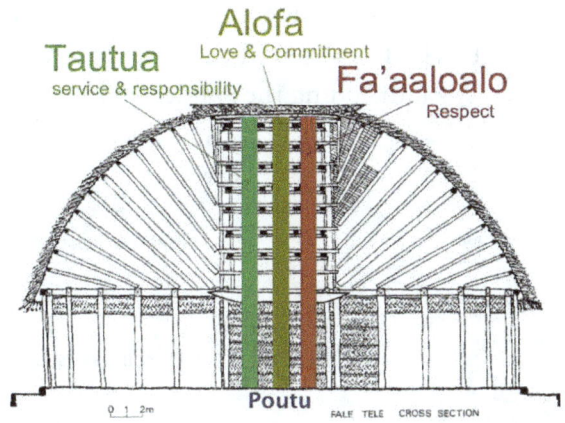

Source: Samu (as cited in Podmore, with Wendt Samu, 2006, p. 38).

Subsequently these three values became the guiding principles of teaching and learning at the centre. Teachers and children use the physical structure of the *fale* (house) for *lotu* (prayers) and group gatherings within the centre to enhance the core values of the *poutu* model (Figure 5.1).

Acknowledging and valuing these overarching principles, the next diagram maps out the focus and direction of the subsequent research journey. The current project's three research questions mark the pointers on this blended model (Figure 5.2). The researchers blended the *poutu* model with the centre's cultural metaphor of *pe'ape'a* (or propeller; i.e. the flax model / A'oga logo) as a philosophical basis to guide the research. By blending the *poutu* principles and the *pe'ape'a* vision, the researchers aimed to support and empower the teachers and parents during the process of responding, in the language(s) of their choice (English/Samoan), to the questionnaires and the focus group questions.

The blended model also enhances the meanings of *poutu*. First, it refers to the strong, supporting structure of the *fale*. The other *poutu* in the centre—the teachers, who are all women—are the strength and the backbone of the centre. Utumapu (1998) noted the significant contribution of women in Samoan language ECE centres, describing the women as *poutu*, reflecting their strength and the strength of their families, churches and communities. The Samoan saying "E au le ina'ilau a tama'ita'i" ("The legacy of women is one of total achievement")[1] is reflected in the teachers' roles and strengths, not only in the running of the centre but as ongoing knowledge seekers and researchers. The teacher-researchers involved in this project consulted with the whole team at the A'oga, including the children and their parents.

Figure 5.2: An overview of the blended cultural framework for this research: poutu and pe'ape'a

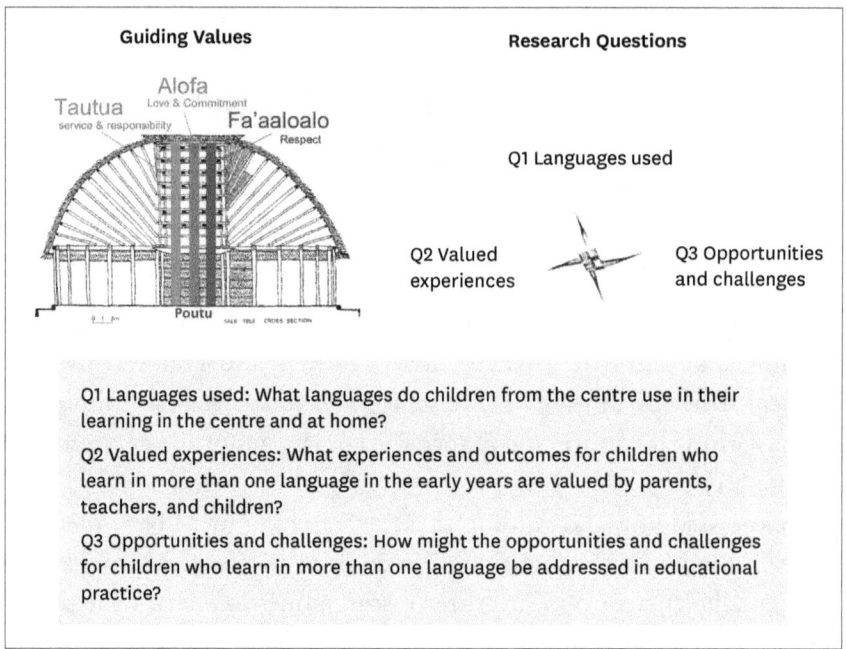

Q1 Languages used: What languages do children from the centre use in their learning in the centre and at home?

Q2 Valued experiences: What experiences and outcomes for children who learn in more than one language in the early years are valued by parents, teachers, and children?

Q3 Opportunities and challenges: How might the opportunities and challenges for children who learn in more than one language be addressed in educational practice?

The weaving process of the principles of love, respect and service with the pe'ape'a is ongoing. Three pointers of the pe'ape'a represented the three research questions guiding this research, and the fourth pointer represented the centre's future aspirations and dreams. A pathway towards fulfilling such dreams and aspirations is identified in the findings of this research.

Research participants

The A'oga Fa'a Samoa was one of four ECE centres participating in this research, and as explained fully in Chapter 3, data generation processes used at each of the centres included: a teacher and a parent questionnaire, one teacher focus group and one parent focus group, interviews with children, observations during arrivals and departures at the centre, videoed observations of learning and teaching interactions, and a video clip of children and teachers during group activities / mat times (e.g. in the *fale* at the A'oga). We now outline some details specific to the A'oga Fa'a Samoa centre's participating teachers, parents and children.

Teachers

Two teachers in the A'oga Fa'a Samoa were New Zealand born and the rest were all Samoan born. Twelve teachers completed teacher questionnaires in English, and 11 of them also participated in the teacher *fono* / focus group. The researchers conducted the teacher *fono* / focus group in Samoan. Transcribed notes were analysed in Samoan before they were translated into English.

Parents

Thirty-five parents from diverse backgrounds completed questionnaires in English. Seven of these parents also participated in the parents' focus group, including two couples. Overall, five families were represented in the parents' *fono* / focus group.

To represent the diversity within the centre, teachers selected the focus group parents from different language backgrounds. Several parents spoke languages other than Samoan in the home (e.g. Tongan, Japanese and Māori). They were from ethnically mixed-marriage families and their partners were Samoan. Teachers also chose one parent who had recently arrived from Samoa and was strong in her Samoan language at home, and New Zealand-born Samoan parents who were at different levels of Samoan language abilities and used both English and Samoan at home. Parents who participated in the focus group were:

- a New Zealand-born Tongan mother who spoke mainly Tongan and preferred to speak Tongan in the home—her Samoan husband spoke Samoan with their children (Parent 1)
- a Japanese mother who spoke Japanese with her children—the children understood her Japanese but responded in English; her husband, who also participated in the focus group, was a New Zealand-born Samoan and spoke Samoan and English to their children (Parents 2 and 3)

- a New Zealand-born Samoan parent who spoke primarily English to the children (Parent 4)
- a father who spoke "50 percent English and 50 percent Samoan"—his New Zealand-born Samoan wife also participated, and she, too, spoke English and Samoan with their children (Parents 5 and 6)
- a Samoan-born parent who spoke entirely Samoan with the children (Parent 7).

A Samoan-born father who spoke Samoan and English in the home, and whose wife spoke Māori fluently in the home, was unable to attend the focus group but was interviewed separately.

Children

Teacher-researchers conducted short interviews in Samoan with six children. The interviews were transcribed and later translated into English.

Findings

Research question 1: What languages do children from participating ECE centres use in their learning in the centre and at home?

Questionnaire findings on parents' and teachers' reported proficiency in speaking Samoan are summarised in Figure 5.3 below. This indicates that almost all of the teachers were fluent speakers of Samoan and could carry out long conversations with adults, whereas fewer than 30 percent of the parents responded that they could carry out long conversations with adults in Samoan.

Figure 5.3: A'oga Fa'a Samoa parents' and teachers' Samoan language proficiency as a percentage

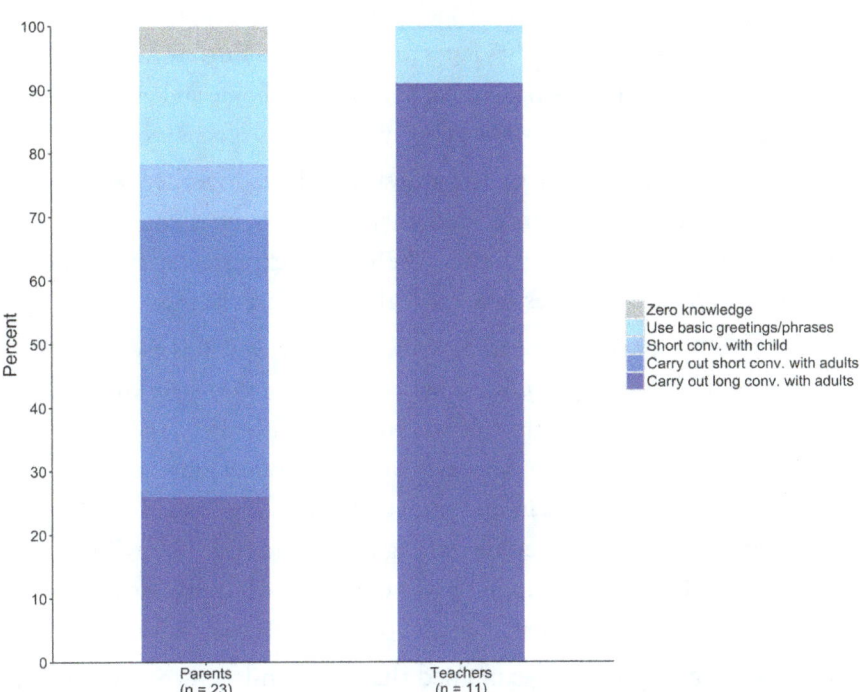

Questionnaires and video observations confirmed that in the centre teachers spoke Samoan and the children spoke both Samoan and English. Teachers in the focus group noted that when a group of children were speaking English, the teacher would respond entirely in Samoan. In the video clips in the context of mat times the children mainly used the Samoan language to talk, recite and interact. Observations of arrival and departure times showed that, along with Samoan and English, one Japanese, one Tongan and three Māori parents regularly used their heritage/home languages with their own children.

Teachers in the focus group reported that in the home, children used both Samoan and English, and some used other home languages. Focus group parents discussed how they valued using Samoan in the home, stating that they actively encouraged their children to speak Samoan. Several parents explained why they spoke Samoan at home and described their experiences speaking Samoan with their children:

> For me I speak 100 percent Samoan at home to my children because they are from Samoa they are trying to pick up their English as well, but it's funny like my little one, when I spoke to him in Samoan, he responds back in English, so I know it's faster to catch up the English … but I'm still continuing to speaking to them in Samoan at home and everywhere we go … Samoan is the first language, yes. (Parent 7, focus group)

Many parents' responses to the questionnaires, together with some focus group comments, indicated that they felt challenged to learn more Samoan. For some parents, the child's experience at the A'oga strengthened their own resolve to speak Samoan at home.

> For myself I speak in Samoan most of the time to my kids even though it['s] probably not fluent but … ever since they were young, when we came to A'oga the rule was you speak at home … so I've been speaking Samoan to them ever since they were young, so but now that [older child] is in first year at school his English is actually getting really good, so they are starting to respond back in English, and I'm still trying to work out a way to make them speak back to me in Samoan, because I know they can. (Parent 3, focus group)

Some focus group parents explained that their children sometimes corrected the way they used Samoan at home. This was the experience of one couple who spoke primarily English at home. They actively encouraged their children to speak Samoan, particularly to their older relatives.

> We try to speak Samoan as best we can as often as we can, but one of the challenges I have [is] if I can't get it right in my head then I don't want to say it because I don't want to speak to him and speak incorrectly … Anyway he corrects me often, which is terrible, it's interesting, but English is a big thing in the home, so for us, both of us, … we speak Samoan as much as we can and certainly when we have my father in town or the relatives, I absolutely encourage them to speak Samoan and a lot of them want to, particularly … my father's generation that they want to speak to the kids, they want to converse with them. It's exciting to get them to speak Samoan. (Parent 4, focus group)

These parents felt challenged to learn more Samoan: "It's really up to us to learn better and faster … We need to improve our education ourselves" (Parent 4, focus group).

Observations and child interviews provided further insights about languages spoken at the A'oga or at home. Teachers and children had some sustained conversations about languages spoken. This is a brief excerpt:

Teacher:	Ae a pe a e alu i le fale, e tautala oe fa'asamoa? (Do you speak Samoan at home?)
Child:	Ioe. (Yes.)
Teacher:	Ia ai? (To whom?)
Child:	I le tama ma le tina o a'u. (To my dad and mum.)
Teacher:	E tautala fa'asamoa outou? (Oh, do you speak in Samoan?)
Child:	Ioe. (Yes.)
Teacher:	Ae a ia lou Nana? (What about your Nana?)
Child:	E tautala palagi. (She speaks English.)
Teacher:	A talanoa la oe i lou Nana e fa'apalagi pe fa'asamoa? (So what language do you use when talking to her?)
Child:	E fa'asamoa. (Samoan.)
Teacher:	E malamalama lou Nana, oi ae a tali mai e fa'apalgi? (Oh, so your Nana understands Samoan but replies in English?)
Child:	Ioe. (Yes.)

The example of the teacher–child interview above showed that the child spoke Samoan in the home but his grandmother used English. It was evident that the language children learned through participation at the A'oga was transferrable to the context of the *aiga* and/or extended fanau.

Research question 2: What experiences and outcomes for children who learn in more than one language in the early years are valued by parents, teachers and children?

The analyses of the focus group interviews and the questionnaire data showed considerable consistency of experiences and outcomes valued by teachers and parents. Teachers valued the Samoan language and described how parents valued their heritage/home languages. Teachers also valued partnerships with and support from parents, especially the parents' encouragement for their children to continue using Samoan in the home.

Focus group parents' comments on children's experiences and the learning outcomes they valued were sorted into key themes. Further scrutiny across all the data showed that these key themes were also supported by the questionnaire responses, video observations and child interview data.

1. Holistic development, including spirituality and identity

Findings within this theme were consistent with the *holistic development* principle of *Te Whariki*, the New Zealand early childhood curriculum (Ministry of Education, 1996). Parents' comments endorsed the centre practices that reflected the principle of holistic development.

Several children who were interviewed indicated strong Samoan identity, and they also enjoyed learning through Samoan. A brief example was:

Teacher:	E fiafia oe e tautala fa'asamoa? (Do you like speaking Samoan?)
Child:	Ioe. (Yes.)
Teacher:	Aisea? (Why?)
Child:	E fiafia e alu i le a'oga, e fiafia e ta'alo i le A'oga fa'asamoa. (I like going to A'oga and I like playing there).

The above excerpt of teacher–child dialogue shows a child affirming his enjoyment of speaking Samoan and participating in the Samoan-language immersion programme. It is also an example of how a teacher's use of appropriate questions and prompts ("Why?") challenged the child's thinking and extended his length of utterance in Samoan from an initial one-word response to a complete sentence. At this centre, valued holistic learning included learning through the Samoan language and identifying positively with the language and culture.

When asked about their experience of the cultural practices at the A'oga Fa'a Samoa, several parents spoke about what they valued, including experiences of prayers (*lotu*):

> Like saying a prayer before you leave. Yeah, so we make sure we sing the *lotu* before we eat and when we have dinner or breakfast or

> whoever is on the dinner table, we get him to do it, but we all sing it with him … What we found was that, some of his cousins don't know the song, and he gets quite proud, because he knows it and he can sing it. They haven't learnt it … we get him to sing that at home, which he's learnt from here. (Parent 6, focus group)

> At home, my husband always has to say the *lotu* before we eat, so he does it in his own way but as soon as he's finished, my son [aged 2 years] always wants to sing that song, for him to eat … so always every day he wants, even though we did the *lotu*, after that he wants to sing that song. (Parent 7, focus group)

They also valued their children's experiences of celebrations, Christmas carols and plays. The following text demonstrates and explains the lotu (prayer) and group activities in the fale.

Lotu:
O taeao uma e amata ai le a'oga i le lotu, e usu le pese ma fai le tatalo e ta'ita'i e tamaiti, ona fai loa lea o le tauvalaauga. O i, e tuu ai le avanoa i le tamaititi e tu ai i luga, ta'u lona igoa, igoa o ona matua, o ona tausaga ma le a'oga e alu iai.

Group activity in the fale:
Every morning children come together for our morning lotu in our fale. They sing a hymn and say a prayer led by children. Each child is then greeted by name and given the opportunity to stand up and say his/her name, his/her parents' names, their age, and the centre they attend.
O lo'u igoa o _____ (My name is_____)
O lo'u tama o_____ (My dad is_____)
O lo'u tina o _____(My mum is_____)
E _____ o'u tausaga (I'm _____ years old)
Oute alu i le A'oga Fa'a Samoa, i Richmond Road Primary School.
(I go to A'oga Fa'a Samoa at Richmond Road Primary School.)

Teachers explained that *lotu* practices enhanced *Te Whāriki*'s principle of holistic development. In this centre, holistic learning and development were inclusive of Samoan (heritage/home) language learning, identity development and spirituality.

Parents also valued their children's Samoan identity development, as evidenced in their comments about language, food, and dress code or costumes. For example, one couple spoke of food and cultural costumes:

> Ever since he's worn his ie faikaga [boys' or men's Samoan outfit for special occasions], when we go to church, he always wants to wear ie faikaga … He loves his ie faikaga. He sort of associates that with something special, so every Sunday when we go to church, he has to … and that's one thing that my parents are proud … that you know our little boy always wants to wear ie faikaga.
>
> Another thing is the food that we eat … that you guys introduce them to, is all part of the learning response, so I think that is one cultural thing and the dress … the ie faikaga. And he knows that it's special occasions that he wears … so after church, we get home and [he] takes it off and puts it away not like his other clothes, just chucks [them] everywhere he doesn't really care, there's no significance about it, whereas the ie faikaga, there's … it's important to him.
>
> What's even worse, when I don't want to wear ie faikaga, he makes me wear ie faikaga like … I'll come dressed in the pants and shirt, 'Dad … ie faikaga, ie faikaga'. Yeah, so I guess that's really good, something that he's picked up from the A'oga. (Parents 5 and 6, focus group)

The couple considered that there were connections between their child's valuing specific cultural practices, such as dress and food, and his strong self-esteem.

Parents also described how their children who had attended the A'oga had learned to respect their elders. The elders actively acknowledged the children and their efforts to use Samoan in the home, as one parent commented:

> Just recently I've noticed, the older son, he knows the difference between Tongan and Samoan. Before we eat, he'll look around and where he's at, he'll say the prayer according to the culture. If we are at [the father's] Samoan family, he'll say it in Samoan. Nana really appreciates it because she doesn't speak English and I just think that [him] being the oldest, I'm kinda proud that he's got that aspect of his Samoan culture. (Parent 1, focus group)

The theme of holistic learning and development was similarly evident across the questionnaires completed by the wider group of parents. Learning experiences and outcomes that parents valued and shared were aligned with their focus on academic learning and success. In other words, parents valued not only the Samoan language, cultural practices, spirituality, respect, identity and wellbeing, but they also wished for and valued academic success for their children.

2. Valuing the power of the Samoan language

Discussions with parents highlighted Cummins's (2000, 2001a, 2001b, 2009) suggestions about ways teachers could support parents to overcome emotional experiences caused by the power of the dominant language within the context of minority groups such as Samoans in Aotearoa New Zealand. Parents commented on how their experiences of the colonisation of language (i.e. historical pressure to use English only) had reminded them to recognise and reactivate what they had lost. Parents continued to value the Samoan language, and to encourage their own children to speak Samoan in the home, as this parent noted:

> I've been brought up without the language. I had to teach myself, and I so know the importance of them actually replying in Samoan, because I know that if they don't reply in Samoan, they will be pretty much be like how I was—you understand it, but you can't speak it—so I'm still working out a way to motivate them to be able to respond in Samoan. (Parent 3, focus group)

Another parent shared her story:

> When we first came from Samoa, I was 4 years old and my little brother was 2 years old. Our parents did not allow us to speak Samoan at home. It's because we … they wanted us to learn English, they didn't feel it was important for us to know Samoan back then. It wasn't until my teenage years that I … decided to get back into my Samoan, but it was new for my mum and dad … [I] started encouraging [them] to speak Samoan to my son because they've been so used to us speaking English. Even though they could speak Samoan, we just have to remind them, 'Oh mum speak Samoan to [child's name] please,' because they speak English and now started getting used to it. Yeah, that's sort of what I've noticed ever since

> [child] has been coming to A'oga. We've encouraged our family and friends to speak Samoan. (Parent 5, focus group)

Valuing the non-coercive power of the Samoan language was important, and is consistent with Cummins's (2000) suggestion that the heritage/home language needs to be used positively. Some parents described a tendency to resort to their most familiar language to express anger or "to growl" at their children. One parent commented on this trend, explaining that the more familiar language was Samoan:

> I sometimes have to remind myself to speak Samoan … I guess I always find myself resorting back to English, but I notice that when I get angry or when he's not listening, then I go into Samoan and then he responds. (Parent 5, focus group)

For other parents, the more familiar language was not Samoan, as this parent explained:

> When I get confused or when you get angry, when you get emotional … you tend to resort back to your mother tongue, so I always resort back to English. But luckily I don't get upset that much. I notice that my wife [Parent 2], when she gets angry she starts speaking in Japanese to them and they seem to understand. (Parent 3, focus group)

Valuing a child's heritage/home language and its power implies a need to use the heritage/home language primarily in a positive way. Parents valued the way that, at the A'oga Fa'a Samoa the teachers used the Samoan language positively and constructively to enhance children's learning.

Observations illustrated repeatedly how children spoke in Samoan and valued using the language. Some children also modelled their teachers' use of Samoan and their teaching strategies. In the following excerpt from a video of two girls (Child 1 and Child 2), one child used Samoan to role-play being a teacher. They are joined by a teacher towards the end of this excerpt. Child 1 is pointing to the image of a volcano erupting in a book and says:

Child 1:   Mauga … le mauga mu i fafo. (Volcano … the volcanic eruption out there.)

Child 2:   I luga. (Up there.) [*smiles*]

Child 1:   And i fafo. (And outside.)

Child 2:   [*pause*] Leai (no), this one just do it to the dinosaur … put in …

[Child 1 reaches over and tries to help turn over to the next page]

Child 2:   *[As if she just remembers that she is the teacher and not Child 1.]* What happens here? *[while tapping on a particular image on the page]*

Child 1:   Leai se mauga mu. (No volcanic eruption.)

Child 2:   Leai se mauga mu i luga. (No volcanic eruption up there.) What happens here?

Child 1:   Ua ai le tainasoa i le laau. (The dinosaur is eating the tree.)

Child 2:   *[Pause]* Manaia (good) *[as she slowly turns to the next page]*.

Child 1:   Ua tagi le tinasoa. (The dinosaur is crying.)

Teacher: Aisea ua tagi ai le tainasoa? (Why did the dinosaur cry … why?)

This excerpt illustrates how the older child used questions and praise, and the children corrected each other by restating the answers using the correct words in Samoan. The teacher who later joined the girls similarly used questions. The teacher noted that these teaching strategies of questioning, restatement and expansion, praise, and role modelling were consistent with an additive approach to bilingualism and with Baker's (2011) work on effective, facilitative pedagogical practices with bilingual and multilingual learners.

3. Metalinguistic awareness

During focus group discussions, parents and teachers commented on their young bilingual children's receptivity to other languages, which indicated their metalinguistic awareness. The benefits of bilingualism include heightened awareness of languages, or metalinguistic awareness (Baker, 2011). As in the following example, parents described how their children became aware of, recognised and accepted diverse languages and identities:

> Well, I think it's more about this generation and their access to media ... I find that [our son] compared to some of his *palagi* friends and relatives picks up counting [in Spanish] very quickly and greetings in Spanish very, very quickly and he doesn't recite them, and I think it's a factor of him, which is to be open to learning more languages just by learning two languages [Samoan and English]. Anyway, the way he is developing, means that he is able to absorb the languages as well, so we're not formally trying to teach them stuff, it's just because it's available he can learn faster than other kids do. (Parent 4, focus group)

A Tongan mother also explained:

> When they're learning another language like Samoan, for my kids especially Tongan as well, they get a sense of [identity], they find out who they are and at the same time they realise that there's other people that have a different culture from themselves ... They can see that not everyone is Samoan or Tongan, but when they learn more than just English you think beyond just the English. My son, for example, comes home and says, 'Hey Mum, B ... is Samoan and Japanese ... and he would say someone else is Samoan and Niuean. So it's more social skills, just accepting others. It's let's acknowledge other people and appreciate that ... they appreciate their Samoan speaking more than one language. (Parent 1, focus group)

Parents valued Samoan language and cultural practices at the A'oga Fa'a Samoa. For example, one parent described an incident when he was crossing the road with his young child:

> I remembered the song "Va'ai le taumatau, va'ai le agavale" then [the child] sang along too, and asked, 'What does natinati loa mean? a? natinati loa?' And I said ... 'Look left, right'. We've done that a few times when we've gone for a walk and when he gets into that song. (Parent 5, focus group)

In this way a road safety song was put into practice. Metalinguistic awareness was apparent in children's transferring of the Samoan language and concepts from the centre to their home and/or community.

4. Transferring of languages

One highly valued outcome of children's learning was transferring and/or applying Samoan language use from the A'oga Fa'a Samoa immersion setting (and from the bilingual Samoan class at school) to the community and/or extended *fanau* contexts. Less fluent speakers of Samoan described how their own heritage/home language became enriched in tandem with their children's learning, thereby reversing a generational trend of language loss. For example, one parent, talking about reading bedside stories to their child, explained:

> It's good for me because I am learning how to pronounce the words, based on the story, because I take on the character—Aunty Mele and Uncle Jerome—and people like that. It's great, they enjoy it. That story time is so important for them. (Parent 4, focus group)

Research question 3: How might the opportunities and challenges for children who learn in more than one language be addressed in educational practice?

Parents' views about educational aspirations, and their priorities for their children, suggested both opportunities and challenges for educational practice. Overall, parents' main hopes for their young children were to be:

- well-grounded in their Samoan language, culture, and values
- respectful
- bilingual in Samoan and English, or multilingual
- healthy

and at the same time:

- to achieve academically.

For example, comments made by 23 parents who completed questionnaires included:

> The most important thing that I believe is to understand and communicate with others in both English and Samoan (Parent 01, questionnaire)

> Knowledge of Samoan culture and language, understand their own heritage and be proud of it, be able to communicate effectively with other family members in Samoa. (Parent 03, questionnaire)

> How to communicate in the languages spoken and written and an appreciation for cultural diversity and to respect it. (Parent 04, questionnaire)

> Understanding their culture, who they are as individuals and how their talents, skills, and voice can contribute to a positive and safe community [in] which they live, respect for others, environment and themselves. To understand they are loved, and supported to then feel encouraged to strive for what they believe. To know who they are and where they've come from is important. (Parent 05, questionnaire)

> Understand and speak Samoan. To learn aspects of fa'a Samoa e.g. respect, love. To work hard. Be respectful, be true to oneself. To always give something 100 percent and never give up. Education and hard work is the key to success. (Parent 14, questionnaire)

> Learning their culture and language so they can be proud of where they come from. (Parent 18, questionnaire)

> Creativity. Self-driven. Problem solvers. Resilience. It's important they have a strong sense of self, who they are, where they come from. (Parent 22, questionnaire)

Parents' views and experiences, expressed both in the questionnaires and in focus group responses, clearly endorsed the immersion policies and practices of the A'oga Fa'a Samoa. Parents' aspirations for their children offered challenges to children, teachers and educational systems. A key challenge was to enact and support holistic learning in the heritage/home language, and academic achievement, guided by cultural values.

- Teachers identified the overarching key opportunities and challenges for educational practice arising from this research as:
- providing additional Samoan language support for children and their families
- keeping children's learning and assessment records entirely in Samoan, the heritage/home language
- empowering parents by involving them in the programme
- celebrating identities—"being Samoan [and other cultural and ethnic identities]".

During the process of the research at the A'oga Fa'a Samoa, the teacher-researchers worked alongside three university researchers to identify, analyse and reflect on the key themes arising from the data. Although challenging, this research process provided teachers with an opportunity to examine their practices further, with reference to relevant research literature on bilingualism.

Teacher-researchers contributed to discussions with the researchers about using the heritage/home language in a positive way with young children to extend their learning. Teachers noted that the results of the research encouraged them to continue and extend their Samoan-language immersion practices, and that an ongoing challenge for the centre was to encourage children to transition to the bilingual Samoan class in the primary school to maintain and extend their Samoan language competence.

Teachers' reflections at the conclusion of the research included this one: "I think something we got from the research is the power of language, how we need to teach the children [entirely] in Samoan, and that scolding [using the heritage/home language] is not needed". Teachers cited this Samoan proverb:

E logo i tino matagi lelei.
(It is sweeter for one's ears to hear pleasant words than bad ones.)

Conclusions

The research findings at the A'oga Fa'a Samoa exemplified an additive approach to bilingualism in action within a language-immersion setting. The influence of the theoretical idea of funds of knowledge was evident. The values that underpinned the research at the A'oga Fa'a Samoa, together with the emergent key themes, suggest opportunities, challenges and key issues for teachers and parents in educational practice. These values, and some key issues and aspirations, are depicted in Figure 5.4.

Figure 5.4: Blended model depicting values, and some key issues and aspirations for young children learning at the A'oga Fa'a Samoa

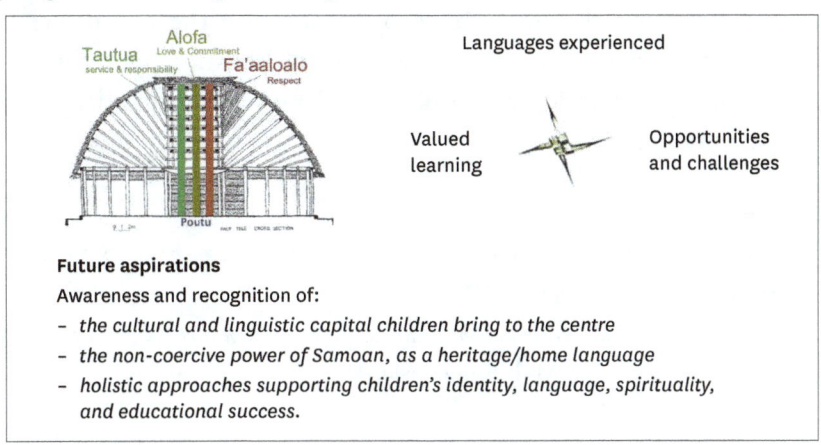

Future aspirations
Awareness and recognition of:
- *the cultural and linguistic capital children bring to the centre*
- *the non-coercive power of Samoan, as a heritage/home language*
- *holistic approaches supporting children's identity, language, spirituality, and educational success.*

Taking the values of *alofa* (love and commitment), *tautua* (service and responsibility) and *fa'aaloalo* (respect) further, teachers reflected on implications from the research findings. In the same way that the *poutu* (posts) at the centre of a *fale* (house) are unmoved, fixed features, the values of *alofa* (love and commitment), *tautua* (service and responsibility) and *fa'aaloalo* (respect) remain constant. Teachers considered that these values will continue to guide the teaching, learning and research at the A'oga Fa'a Samoa.

In contrast, the *pe'ape'a* (propeller) rotates. It moves by wind, guided by where the wind comes from—by the direction and strength of the wind. Teachers interpreted the symbolism of the *pe'ape'a* as meaning that ongoing learning evolves, as in this study, with new knowledge and new directions for children and teachers.

The new findings from this study showed how acceptance of the cultural and linguistic capital that children bring to the centre, recognition of the non-coercive power of the heritage/home language, and holistic approaches support children's learning. For teachers who work in language and cultural immersion settings, this type of values-oriented model may potentially provide a pathway towards supporting young children who learn in more than one language, in partnership with their families.

In summary, this chapter explored young children's experiences of languages within the A'oga Fa'a Samoa and in their homes. The findings showed how parents appreciated that, within the centre, teachers spoke entirely in Samoan and supported the children to learn through Samoan. The chapter reported parents', teachers' and children's perspectives on learning experiences and outcomes that they valued. Key findings supported the importance of recognising the non-coercive power of the heritage/home language, and of holistic approaches to teaching to support children's developing identities and their learning through Samoan.

References

Baker, C. (2011). *Foundations of bilingualism and bilingual education* (5th ed.). Clevedon, UK: Multilingual Matters.

Cummins J. (2000). *Language, power and pedagogy: Bilingual children in the crossfire*. Clevedon, UK: Multilingual Matters.

Cummins, J. (2001a). HER Classic Empowering Minority students: Framework for intervention. Author's introduction. *Harvard Educational Review, 71*(4), 649–655.

Cummins, J. (2001b). *Negotiating identities: Education for empowerment in a diverse society* (2nd ed.) Los Angeles, CA: California Association for Bilingual Education.

Cummins, J. (2009). Pedagogies of choice: Challenging coercive relations of power in classrooms and communities. *International Journal of Bilingual Education and Bilingualism, 12*(30), 261–271. doi: 10.1080/136700509/03003751

Ministry of Education. (1996). *Te whāriki: He whāriki mātauranga mō ngā mokopuna o Aotearoa: Early childhood curriculum.* Wellington: Learning Media. Retrieved from http://www.education.govt.nz/early-childhood/teaching-and-learning/ece-curriculum/

Podmore, V. N., with Wendt Samu, T. (2006). *O le tama ma lana a'oga, O le tama ma lona fa'asinomaga: Nurturing positive identity in children: Final research report from the A'oga Fa'a Samoa, an Early Childhood Centre of Innovation.* Wellington: Ministry of Education. Retrieved from http://www.educationcounts.govt.nz/publications/ece/22551/22555

Taouma, J., Tapusoa, E., & Podmore, V. N. (2013). Nurturing positive identity in children: Action research with infants and young children at the A'oga Fa'a Samoa, an early childhood Centre of Innovation. *Journal of Educational Leadership Policy and Practice, 28*(1), 50–59.

Tuafuti, P. (2010). Pasifika additive bilingual education: Unlocking the culture of silence. *MAI Review, 1.* Retrieved from http://www.review.mai.ac.nz/index.php/MR/issue/view/15

Tuafuti, P., & McCaffery, J. (2005). Family and community empowerment through bilingual education. *International Journal of Bilingual Education and Bilingualism, 8*(5), 1–24. doi: 10.1080/13670050508668625

Utumapu, T. L. P. (1998). *O le poutu: Women's roles and Samoan language nests.* Unpublished doctoral thesis, University of Auckland.

Acknowledgements

We warmly acknowledge Dr Diane Mara, who contributed to the earlier stages of this research.

We also acknowledge Dr Tanya Wendt Samu's work. Her *poutu* model depicting values for research remains inspirational (Samu, 2005, as cited in Podmore with Wendt Samu, 2006).

We also thank Makerita Atonio, who transcribed and translated interview data, analyses and video clips while working as a summer scholar at the University of Auckland, supervised by Dr Peter Keegan and Associate Professor Helen Hedges.

Endnotes

1 This bracketed translation is by Vaimasenuu Zita Martel. Eneleata Tapusoa's further explanation of the background "story" is: There was a house built in one of the villages in Savai'i. The only part that was completed was the part that was done by women. Hence the saying, "E au le ina'ilau a tama'ita'i" referring to the resilience of women and how they will not give up until something is done.

Chapter 6 Multilingual children, multilingual teachers: Symonds Street Early Childhood Education Centre

Thirumagal Anandh, Nola Harvey and Helen Hedges; with Auemetua Lotomau and Ruwinaaz Subhani

Toku reo, toku akatika, toku akaaraara.
Apii ia, tamou ia, o'oraia kite ao.
Kia kore e ngaro.[1]
My language, my reality, my awakening.
Learn a language, nurture it, share it with the world
to keep it from extinction.

Introduction

In an English-medium setting where both children and teachers are multilingual, children may not share a common language apart from learning in English together. Symonds Street is located in the central city of Auckland on a main arterial route that bisects the University of Auckland campus. The street acts as a main thoroughfare for children, students and staff as they move between the early childhood centre, lecture and study facilities. Auckland's super-diversity status (Royal Society of New Zealand, 2013) is well evidenced in the many languages and cultures participating in this university community. Just a few metres back from the street, at the entrance to the Symonds Street Early Childhood Centre, parents, children and teachers exchanged greetings and farewells in 16 different languages at the time of the research, a rich microcosm of the university community it serves. This chapter examines the centre context and philosophy, and the participants in the project, and reports the findings related to the research questions.

Centre context and philosophy

The Symonds Street Early Childhood Centre is one of the University of Auckland's six early childhood centres. It is a sessional ECE centre, licensed for 36 children aged 2½ to 5 years. It provides early childhood services largely for postgraduate students and a few staff of the University of Auckland. Children attend the centre to suit parents' and partners' research, study and teaching commitments rather than for a full day. Special characteristics of this centre include responsiveness to the university semester schedule and the more flexible requirements of doctoral students. Many students are transnationals, in Aotearoa New Zealand to study for a short period before returning to their country of origin. The majority of families identified affiliations with a range of Asian language, culture and ethnic groupings from Malaysia, Indonesia, Japan, China, Sri Lanka, India and Korea. At the time of the research there was a team of seven bilingual or multilingual teachers; six were qualified and registered. The centre is therefore English-medium, but strongly and proudly a multilingual and multi-ethnic centre.

The centre's philosophy fosters respect for diverse religious protocols and acknowledges cultural festivals in order to embrace and celebrate cultural, social and language diversity among the tamariki, whānau and community. The teachers' shared philosophy statement during the period of the research included:

- viewing each child as a unique, capable and competent learner
- respecting the role of parents as the child's first teacher

- sustaining a close partnership with parents
- believing that the principle of ako (learners as teachers and teachers as learners) underpins all pedagogical practices
- acknowledging Māori as tangata whenua (the first and indigenous peoples) of Aotearoa New Zealand and upholding the principles of partnership central to Te Tiriti o Waitangi
- respecting and valuing Aotearoa New Zealand as a bicultural nation that embraces a diverse and multicultural society
- recognising that each person in our community of learners brings a special history/herstory, with cultural influences that will continue to inform personal and collective knowledge of understanding
- following the principles, strands and goals of *Te Whāriki* (Ministry of Education, 1996) as a guide to action beliefs
- nurturing each child's knowledge of her/his own culture and world views to build self-esteem and identity as capable and competent contributors to society
- responding with respect and dignity to each child and family.

Participants in the research

Teachers

All seven teachers completed the questionnaire and six participated in the teacher focus group. Questionnaire findings showed teachers spoke 12 languages: English, te reo Māori, Cook Island Māori, Tongan, Samoan, Tamil, Sinhalese, Urdu, Hindi, Arabic, Malayalam and Telugu. The teacher focus group was held at the centre in the early evening and was conducted in English.

Parents

Twenty-seven parents completed the questionnaire in English. For the parent focus group, teachers approached parents who used their heritage/home language/s. Further criteria were parents' availability during university examination time and representation of diverse languages. Four parents, all mothers of children at the centre, participated. Languages from Korea, Japan, Indonesia and Chile were represented. The focus group was held during the morning, in a meeting room on the city campus, at a time that suited the four participants.

Children

Forty-one children attended the centre at the time of the research. More than half of the children enrolled were emerging bilinguals, accustomed to using their heritage/home language only, and were learning English in the centre. Teacher-researchers completed interviews with six children. Teacher–child interview pairs were selected according to the teacher's fluency in the child's heritage/home language, and each interview was undertaken in that language. During the research period several of the children left to attend English-medium schools in Auckland, visited families in their home countries for several weeks, or returned with families to their home countries to attend school or kindergarten. This illustrates that children are expected by their families to become bilingual or multilingual in order to negotiate multiple contexts.

Findings

Research question 1: What languages do children from participating ECE centres use in their learning in the centre and at home?

Field note observations of arrivals and departures revealed a mix of heritage/home languages and English spoken by parents and children. Between them more than half of the 41 families sustained 16 heritage/home languages. Twelve spoke English, two te reo Māori, five Malay, four Japanese, three Urdu, three Indonesian, two Korean, two Arabic, and one each spoke Farsi, Malayalam, Mandarin, Russian, Sinhalese, Spanish, Swedish and Tagalog. Teachers interacted with the children in English, used greetings in as many heritage/home languages as possible, and prioritised non-verbal communication strategies to support initial meaning making until children were more familiar with English.

Cultural protocols and respectful, culturally appropriate greetings and farewells occurred between teachers and parents who shared common languages. Some children followed their parents' example and used referential greetings and gestures appropriately with teachers. Of the 28 parents who greeted their children in their heritage/home language at departure time, half responded comfortably in their heritage/home language and the remainder responded to their parents in English. In addition, children who shared a language in common used their heritage/home language in play and for friendships. Otherwise, children attempted to communicate in English, and in doing so improved their English language learning alongside other learning.

During the teacher focus group one teacher commented on her use of her own heritage/home language in the centre.

> I use it [heritage/home language] throughout the day. ... mother comes and speaks to me in Urdu. So when I speak to them they're quite expert in Urdu, so I'm quite conscious of my language skills. But most ... [often when] they [parents] have a concern that they want to come and talk about, they usually speak in Urdu ... I think they can relate more ... because it is easy to explain in Urdu. (Teacher 2, focus group)

This teacher identified that the use of heritage/home languages was particularly important when parents were revealing children's health issues to teachers. She recounted that a relieved mother had commented in Urdu, "Oh I didn't know how to say it. I was worried that you would put him out of the centre."

At the parent focus group each mother shared her distinct approaches to sustaining heritage/home languages and English as they supported their children to learn in more than one language. The Korean-born mother, who had taken up doctoral studies after her move to Aotearoa New Zealand 6 years earlier, noted that her child preferred to use English initially.

> My husband is a New Zealander ... I started speaking in Korean ... at the beginning she [daughter] got quite frustrated, especially when she went to kindergarten. So ... I avoided speaking in Korean ... but nowadays she likes to show off that she can speak Korean so she has more interest. So I'm starting to speak Korean [again]. (Parent 1, focus group)

The Japanese mother who spoke in Japanese to both her children noted that although her Aotearoa New Zealand-born husband spoke English only with their children, she ensured that her child attended the centre for only 2 days per week so that he would become bilingual.

> I chose day care for only 2 days a week so that I can use Japanese more, and also go to Japanese play groups too and then he [son] can find Japanese friends too. (Parent 2, focus group)

Two parents at the focus group valued the fact that their children had the opportunity to attend community language groups through play groups or church groups to maintain their home languages.

The third participant was an Indonesian mother whose two children had accompanied her and her husband to Aotearoa New Zealand 10 months earlier when he took up his postgraduate studies. She noted that the family had not used English with their children before their arrival. Although she was delighted that her children had acquired English easily in Aotearoa New Zealand, she had considerable concerns about how the children would be able to sustain English and be able to learn in Indonesian again on their return.

> We never talk in English in my country because English is [a] third language; [our] first language is Java, then Indonesian and then the third is English. The government does not force the people from Indonesia to talk in English … When we go back to Indonesia how [do I] … make them [her children] learn … two languages … Indonesian and English too? (Parent 3, focus group)

The mother from Chile had accompanied her Argentinian husband to Aotearoa New Zealand and spoke both Spanish and English to their son. Both sets of grandparents lived in Auckland and only spoke in Spanish with their grandchild. The child spoke in Spanish fluently with his parents and grandparents. This participant was also learning Italian at university and commented that she and her child watched Italian cartoons together. The family were still exploring ways to keep both Spanish and English alive in their household.

> We won't pressure him [son] to speak Spanish but we try to encourage him to enjoy the language as much as he can … So I read Spanish a lot to him … We have some zones in the house [where] we speak English in certain places and Spanish in certain places. (Parent 4, focus group)

Research question 2: What experiences and outcomes for children who learn in more than one language in the early years are valued by parents, teachers and children?

Analyses of the teacher and parent focus group interviews and the questionnaire data established four common themes: wellbeing and belonging, relationships and identities, contributing and taking responsibility, and a rich language and cultural environment. These are described below.

1. Wellbeing and belonging

Findings from the parent and teacher focus group showed that parents and teachers all valued experiences that led to children being understood during, participating in and enjoying learning. Responses from the parent questionnaire revealed that every parent wanted their child to be happy and secure and to participate fully in the educational setting. In terms of wellbeing, valued outcomes were expressed as a "confident, sociable and happy child", "developing a good attitude to learning and knowledge", "self-confidence", "to be confident and communicate well", "learn more about play, fun, learning", "happy and a secure child", "good social skills", "wanting many qualities of kindness, compassion and socialise and develop friends."

Transitioning to, and feeling a sense of belonging in, the centre, brought challenges as the children and families were new to Aotearoa New Zealand, to the English language, and to the early childhood environment. One teacher expressed the view that:

> The transitioning time is quite tough for them because they haven't found friends … We find that they are playing by themselves and quite often they cannot say what they want to do like going to the toilet … We are strangers really. (Teacher 5, focus group)

One teacher who shared a common heritage/home language with an unsettled child recounted how frustrated the child became when he was not understood. Speaking to the child in Urdu, the teacher asked, "Why are you angry?" The child replied in Urdu, "Cos no one will understand me" (Teacher 2, focus group).

These examples illustrated the ways that families and children valued children being able to settle comfortably into the centre in order to learn in English and their own heritage/home languages. Both parents and teachers spoke in the focus groups of the value of children experiencing friendships and building strong identities that empowered children's sense of belonging. These views built on the questionnaire responses relating to aspirations for children.

2. Relationships and identities

The findings revealed the extent to which families new to Aotearoa New Zealand welcomed friendships between their children, particularly when they shared a common language or culture. Children's friendships—and subsequently family friendships—generated a sense of community and identity across families.

Field notes and video clips captured the ways that the teaching and learning environment fostered opportunities to develop strong friendships between and across children of the same culture who shared a common language and used it in play. Analysis of a 4-minute video clip enabled teachers to look closely at a common play and settling-in routine of three Japanese boys. The boys moved from a pretend scenario where they were cats who then turned into humans as they took on and explored working theories about their parents' roles. One expressed cultural protocols when he advised the younger child not to put dirty shoes in a bag. The clip also demonstrated the three Japanese boys improving on their ability to code switch when necessary to respond to a teacher in English. This make-believe play offered one example of children who were capable of building strong relationships through friendships. These children were settled, demonstrated strong identities, and made use of the rich multilingual and multicultural context to become competent communicators and learners, consistent with the aspiration statement of *Te Whāriki*.

Parents also valued the experiences that generated friendships within their own languages and cultures so that children built strong identities through the use of their languages and cultures. In relation to these Japanese children, a Japanese parent commented:

> There are four Japanese boys and they are using Japanese and playing together. It was amazing ... About fire engine and policemen, ambulance. Talking and then using blocks, helmet and costumes.
> (Parent 2, focus group)

Field notes recorded that new friendships continued within New Zealand as the host country. For example, families of the same culture who had met at the centre undertook holidays together to strengthen relationships between the families and children.

> And some of our families ... particularly the Malaysian families they know each other really well so they, they've [had] a big holiday together ... six families all went with children and parents hired houses and went somewhere off for days down to the snow. And that was a way of supporting each other and family-wise as well as language-wise.
> (Teacher 1, focus group)

Families in the centre told teachers that families of the same culture often continued their friendships after they had returned to their home countries.

3. Contributing and taking responsibility

In the focus group, teachers reported the valuable contribution of older children who took responsibility for those children newly arrived in New Zealand and at the centre, most often younger children who shared their language and background. This buddying was also documented in learning stories and supported by video observations. Settling the younger children enabled them to learn and later to repeat the pattern of taking responsibility for other newly arriving children. One teacher commented:

> The transitional phase is very important when they are new to the country, new to the centre, we ... introduce them to other children of their own language, that sometimes works. (Teacher 3, focus group)

Field notes indicated many examples of these buddying actions. For example, no teacher in the centre spoke Mandarin, but a Mandarin-speaking 4-year-old girl assisted a 4-year-old boy to transition and settle comfortably. This child then willingly took responsibility to contribute to settling a younger child. A learning story revealed that the new girl was hesitant, doubtful and uncertain about participating in the strange centre environment. The boy moved to her side and spoke a few words in her home language. At this point her face brightened and showed relief. The connection between the two children enabled her to find her place in the centre.

Teachers' notes indicated that the buddy had stepped out of his own play with his friends and came forward each day to be her guide and her translator. The girl's parents stated that she spoke about "her buddy" at home. Later, beyond the settling period, the girl made new friends of her age group and the boy took on the role of one of her many friends. Six months later the girl took on the role of settler, who not only spoke confidently to a new girl but also to the newcomer's parents and grandparents. This relationship was likened to the Māori concept of tuakana teina and reflected the expectations of many cultures in terms of the role of an experienced member of the group taking responsibility for a newcomer to the group.

4. A rich language and cultural environment

The children's daily cross-language and cultural experiences with a diversity of songs, narrative books and experiences were considered valuable learning and teaching experiences by teachers and parents. The centre afforded a rich environment for languages to flourish and children to learn in more than one language. Teachers reiterated that they valued relationships across cultures as a way to encourage acknowledgement, acceptance and respect for other ethnic, religious and cultural groups.

Responses in the parent questionnaire revealed a strong preference for their children to learn English and play with others using English. This was also the assumption that teachers had been working with prior to the study. However, both the questionnaire responses and the parent focus group data also showed that most parents valued the rich multilingual centre environment for their children's experiences, which encouraged the teachers to work with multiple languages further.

> I'm really happy about this day care because everyone [teachers, parents, children] is using [a] different language and the children know everyone is different. (Parent 2, focus group)

On multiple occasions, teacher-researchers reflected on the documentation that provided evidence of the multicultural nature of the centre. Diversity of language, culture, music, literature and art were visible through learning stories and parent contributions to the curriculum. One example was when an Indonesian parent departing to his home country after completion of his studies gave the centre an Indonesian musical instrument (an angklung). With a new appreciation through the findings of the way parents valued multiple language experiences, a teacher-researcher approached another Indonesian parent for advice on the use of the instrument. That parent, and a large group of his fellow Indonesian community members, visited the centre with two big suitcases of musical instruments. Video documentation showed the Indonesian players teaching the children Indonesian songs. In addition, there was a deep sense of pride and shared identity in singing the New Zealand national anthem in te reo Māori accompanied by the angklung. Similarly, other video documentation and learning stories showed a similar event and outcome from a Japanese grandmother teaching children simple Japanese rhymes. As a result of the study, the funds of knowledge of Symonds Street's community members became a major resource for the centre, and the centre became a place for wider reciprocal exchanges with other families in the wider community.

The majority of the parents expressed in the questionnaire the value they placed on the educational culture of play at the centre. Many identified that their children learning respect for others met their valued outcome of acceptance of diversity. One parent went further and commented on an important outcome of the centre experience as providing a non-prejudiced environment: "I don't want my child to be prejudiced ... have any prejudice against any kind of culture ... from very early on" (Parent 3, focus group). Another parent remarked:

> I think it's such an important thing for a nation to have, cos we're [going to] have a generation of people who are multicultural and they can speak more than one language ... because these kids are [going to] be able to do international things, they are more marketable ... It's really amazing. So our goal, at least with our kids, is for them to speak several languages. (Parent 4, focus group)

Research question 3: How might the challenges for children who learn in more than one language be addressed in educational practice?

1. Opportunities

Teachers used their teaching strategies as opportunities to support heritage/home languages when they settled children into the centre. Teachers spoke freely of the teaching strategies they used with new children to support comfortable and respectful transitioning from home to centre. Teachers made an effort to identify accurately the languages and cultures of new children and families attending for the first time, making use of the enrolment procedures to talk in-depth with each new family.

One teacher spoke of building repertoires that she used for non-verbal communication. These were ways of interacting with children when there were no common languages between the teacher and the child. Instead she used "body language connections" (Teacher 2, focus group) while settling children and during transitions. Teachers made use of lists of common words, phrases and sentences obtained from parents to settle children, both as a regular practice and as a way to support each child to become a confident communicator.

As a regular practice, music, rhyme, songs and lullabies were played regularly in the centre. These were non-threatening and enjoyable opportunities where children became teachers of their home languages. Teachers borrowed multilingual and multicultural resources and texts in heritage/home languages from the library. They also invited multilingual local community librarians, teachers, parents and grandparents to share their funds of knowledge.

As the research progressed, teachers equipped themselves with data and deeper knowledge about brain development and the multiple benefits of bilingualism in the early years. Teachers enjoyed discussions with families, and explored strategies for keeping heritage/home languages active, working collaboratively on shared strategies.

For children who learn in more than one language in English-medium settings, many opportunities arise in everyday centre practices. One of the major opportunities was that parents and children alike enjoyed the multicultural nature of the centre community.

> The other thing is the natural interaction with the other cultures because of the diversity within the centre … he sees his class mates eating that [different] food and it's normal for him … they interact with kids of different cultures and languages. It's good. (Parent 4, focus group)

The teacher focus group responses provided evidence that the teaching team as a whole supported each other to sustain the bilingual/multilingual interactions. Teachers sharing their own cultural heritage provided an opportunity for children and parents to feel comfortable sharing their cultural heritages. Further, teachers' modelling of bilingualism became an invitation for children and parents to share their cultural and languages practices and stimulated a willingness to share their own funds of knowledge.

> Recently … we celebrated Cook Islands language week … I wore a flower in my ear … I translated "Baa Baa Black Sheep" into Cook Island [Māori] and "Little Bird Sits on the Tree" … we made a umu [earth oven] as in the Cook Islands. (Teacher 5, focus group)

Teachers' use of children's heritage/home languages therefore appeared to endorse children's and families' identities. Findings from video observations showed ways that parents, grandparents, whānau and community members made valuable contributions to the daily programme as they shared histories, music and cultural treasures.

Field notes documented further opportunities for children learning in more than one language that arose when bilingual parents translated and read aloud in their heritage/home language from the centre's English story books. Regardless of the language being used on each occasion, many children would gather eagerly around the story reader, listening with interest. This regular exposure to a range of languages fostered children's interest in each other's languages and stimulated inquiry and discussion about languages in what appeared to be growing metalinguistic awareness. This aligned well with parents' valued outcomes for their children to be "well socialised, tolerant … and comfortable in a range of cultures" (Parent questionnaire).

One parent in the focus group appreciated that the "Global Whānau Board" (a map of the world with children's photos pinned to their home country) enabled discussion to be stimulated among teachers and parents about homelands, languages and cultures. In turn, children heard these conversations and had their sense of belonging in several places affirmed. In this way their multiple identities were recognised and fostered.

> I had noticed that teachers put the map of the world and they put the photo of the kids, where they came from and it's great that … kids realise that they are not all living in New Zealand. They are living in different parents of the world. And they have different food, culture and languages. (Parent 1, focus group)

The challenges children experienced related to transitioning into an English-medium setting appeared to create an opportunity to strengthen a culture of respect for, and contributions of, funds of knowledge among teachers. Parents' valued outcomes aligned well with an expectation set out in the philosophy, which was to respond sensitively to each child.

One example of a sensitive response occurred when an Urdu-speaking child from Pakistan was puzzled by a teacher's response to a picture he sketched during one of their regular walks to Auckland City Square. The teacher informed an Urdu-speaking teacher that she could not understand the child's explanation. The Urdu-speaking teacher asked the child what he had sketched and he replied, "Oh I drew a snow!" He explained his related working theories about how the clouds make rain and the coldness in Aotearoa New Zealand made the snow, and he appeared very happy when he was understood and saw that his working theories were appreciated by the teacher. This example illustrates the way children moved between and within languages with teachers to facilitate learning and understanding.

Several families noted in the parents' focus group that they valued opportunities to become familiar with te reo Māori. One parent commented that she liked her child "to know more of Māori culture, which is a very important aspect of this country and we value that" (Parent 4, focus group).

Parents had various strategies to support heritage/home languages. For example, the university semester breaks enabled many parents to return regularly to their home country to be immersed in their heritage/home language. Parents also aimed to empower heritage/home language usage by giving children opportunities to attend a local kindergarten while in their home country. One parent commented on the value of her children visiting Japan for 5 weeks or more in that they were compelled to speak in Japanese because their grandparents could not understand English. The parent affirmed that she arranged visits to Japan every year to spend a reasonable time with families and use "No English, only Japanese" (Parent 2, focus group).

Another strategy to maintain the heritage/home language involved specific language-speaking zones at home:

> Well, normally in the kitchen, for example, we speak Spanish all the time 'cos we are in the kitchen and the lounge …[My son's] room is English mostly cause we communicate in English there … teach him the letters, numbers, things like that. … it's more like guidelines than rules. We try to do things flexibly and he can enjoy everything. (Parent 4, focus group)

The most common focus of parents was to provide opportunities to use their heritage/home language in meaningful, enriching and engaging ways. Examples included: regular telephone conversations, Skype conversations to connect with grandparents and relations and families of similar cultures, and going for holiday trips in Aotearoa New Zealand with members of their own language and community groups. These ways contributed to "supporting each other family-wise and language-wise" (Teacher 1, focus group).

The parent questionnaire and focus group comments revealed that parents had an understanding of the important interconnectedness between language and culture. Parents reported attending cultural playgroups to create a context for speaking their heritage/home languages and enrolling children in community sports groups. A teacher commented about one child: "He plays for a Sri Lankan cricket group … mum says that he is picking up Sinhalese" (Teacher 3, focus group).

2. Challenges

Transitioning and settling into both Aotearoa New Zealand and the ECE centre were major challenges that children, parents and teachers faced together. Field note observations revealed—and the teacher focus group findings reiterated—that children new to the country and new to the early childhood environment appeared anxious, frustrated and stressed, especially when there was no one at the centre who understood their home language. A teacher said that a father shared his concern with her for his child: "He [child] will be frustrated because he won't be able to communicate … so he screams out or he is really frustrated. He gets angry" (Teacher 2, focus group).

Despite the diversity of teachers and support for languages in the centre, parents and teachers alike were challenged by a fear of heritage/home language loss for their children. Responses in the parent questionnaire to the two questions regarding parents' hopes and aspirations for children and learning outcomes for children demonstrated that more than half of the parents felt concerned about language expertise and bilingualism.

For example, some parents recounted that despite regular Skype contact with the child's grandparents living in their home country, often their child was unable to understand or communicate in the heritage/home language and therefore avoided these interactions. Rejection of the use of heritage/home language could then happen quickly. One parent recounted her child saying, "No, I don't want to talk to you grandpa … Silly grandma, what are you talking?" (Parent 3, focus group).

Bilingual teachers who themselves had once been new immigrant parents confirmed that the same kind of language loss was happening in their own households: children disengaging themselves from their grandparents and community events and home country contact. One teacher spoke of her own child's lack of interest and confidence in heritage/home language use.

> She wouldn't, she wouldn't even greet people … she stopped talking to her grandparents … because they would speak to her in Tamil and she would have to respond back in Tamil, so now that relationship is … I'm thinking, 'What have I done?' So it's a huge loss for her. She got the English really good with her friends … but along the line she has lost a lot of relationships. (Teacher 2, focus group)

Many parents in the centre who had to return to their home country after completing their studies showed concern about loss of heritage/home language because of the necessary requirements of speaking, writing and reading in a language that enabled their child to fit into the home country educational system. Several families recognised the challenge of cultural and language shifts. A parent voiced her child's intense fear of going back to his country to continue his schooling due to lack of heritage/home language competence. "I'm just afraid [to return]" (Parent 3, focus group).

Conversely, most parents saw English as a prestigious language, particularly for educational purposes and success. While this was a valued outcome, a challenge arose for children because parents spoke in English at home to support transition into the centre at the expense of the heritage/home language. Even those parents who had to return to their home country wanted their children to learn English "fast" and reap the benefits of being in an English-speaking country and gain the benefits associated with English: "Most of the people in my country want to improve their English and then when their English improves they are proud about that" (Parent 3, focus group).

The majority of the parents supported and maintained their heritage/home language and expressed interest in bilingualism and multilingualism. However, the challenge of potential language loss for children in their early years was not fully understood and there was a lack of clarity about which language parents expected children to speak at home or at the centre.

> A lot of time they [children] come in, they think, 'Oh I can't use my language'. Especially parents [who] are saying we want you to learn English. (Teacher 6, focus group)

Teachers reported that children had considerable metalinguistic awareness and recognised which people understood and spoke their language and which did not. Most children chose to use English in the centre, or when unsure remained quiet. Some children selected "secret" times to use heritage/home languages with friends during their play. One teacher commented that initially a small group who shared a language in common enjoyed being cats and always used their heritage/home language out of sight of teachers.

> They used to hide in the boxes every time and speak their language … I just let them speak while I was trying to listen and when they had finished they came out of the box and I said, 'I hear you speaking different language what was that?'. 'I was speaking Chinese, you don't understand.' 'OK, what do you call a cat in your language?' And [child] says, 'I don't want to tell you!' (Teacher 5, focus group)

Conclusion and outcomes

Key themes identified from the parent and teacher focus group meetings were wellbeing and belonging, relationships and identities, contributing and taking responsibilities, and a rich language and cultural environment. During the research we identified many challenges for teachers and children; for example, transitioning and settling, continuing to nurture heritage/home languages and combat the fear of language loss, and children meeting the expectation of two different, distinct educational systems as confident bilingual learners. With these challenges came rich opportunities for children learning in more than one language; for example, opportunities to contribute their expertise as a bilingual, to learn across cultures (including te reo Māori), to be a part of a rich centre community, and for teachers and parents to build together pedagogical knowledge about bilingualism.

The major outcomes and changes at Symonds Street took the form of a shift from an assumption that children came to learn English, with heritage/home languages to be used as a transition tool, to teachers using their heritage/home languages to support all learning and teaching in the English-medium setting to model the value of bi- and multilingualism. The research provided an opportunity to share concerns, misapprehensions and the value of learning and using multiple languages in a primarily English-speaking nation. The research became a catalyst for changes: children settling children who spoke similar languages, languages as a cognitive resource (not just a settling resource), languages as a way for children and families to connect more, and teachers extending the range of languages through learning greetings, simple words, phrases and sentences. The whole community became a wider source of languages for learning, and reciprocal and extended relationships grew.

Through their own personal and professional experience, bilingual teachers have realised the rapidity with which heritage/home languages can be lost. The teachers recognised that if they do not resist language loss their lives may become fragmented, as funds of knowledge can dissipate, threatening the living cultural literature, art, music, painting, architecture and sculpture, and, as a consequence, identities. One teacher-researcher stated that she was

> clouded with nostalgic memories of her rich cultural heritage; reminded of the literature from an age where ancient kings welcomed … [a poet] with open arms, ardently admired his talent and showered him with gold, such was the passion for home language/mother tongue to live and flourish.

The research reawakened the sense of urgency and importance of sustaining the heritage/home languages, cultures and identities through intentionally well-planned strategies in an additive bilingual approach for all children to thrive.

The poet, Bharathidasan, in his Tamil song *Inbath Thamizh*, highlights the importance of his mother tongue. He affirms heritage/home language as a cornerstone of our lives, and identifies language as the water that nurtures the growth of our society. These ideas are in Bharathidasan's Tamil song that concludes this chapter.

இன்பத் தமிழ்

தமிழுக்கும் அமுதென்று பேர் - அந்தத்
தமிழ் இன்பத் தமிழ் எங்கள் உயிருக்கு நேர்!
தமிழுக்கு நிலவென்று பேர் - இன்பத்
தமிழ் எங்கள் சமுகத்தின் விளைவுக்கு நீர்!
தமிழுக்கு மணமென்று பேர் - இன்பத்
தமிழ் எங்கள் வாழ்வுக்கு நிருமித்த ஊர்!
தமிழுக்கு மதுவென்று பேர் - இன்பத்
தமிழ் எங்கள் உரிமைச்செம் பயிருக்கு வேர்!

தமிழ் எங்கள் இளமைக்கு பால் - இன்பத்
தமிழ் நல்ல புகழ்மிக்க புலவர்க்கு வேல்!
தமிழ் எங்கள் உயர்வுக்கு வான் - இன்பத்
தமிழ் எங்கள் அசதிக்குச் சுடர்தந்த தேன்!
தமிழ் எங்கள் அறிவுக்குத் தோள் - இன்பத்
தமிழ் எங்கள் கவிதைக்கு வயிரத்தின் வாள்!
தமிழ் எங்கள் பிறவிக்குத் தாய் -இன்பத்
தமிழ் எங்கள் வளமிக்க உளமுற்ற தீ!

-பாரதிதாசன்

References

Ministry of Education. (1996). *Te whāriki: He whāriki mātauranga mō ngā mokopuna o Aotearoa: Early childhood curriculum.* Wellington: Learning Media. Retrieved from http://www.education.govt.nz/early-childhood/teaching-and-learning/ece-curriculum/

Royal Society of New Zealand. (2013). *Languages in Aotearoa New Zealand.* Wellington: Author. Retrieved from http://www.royalsociety.org.nz/expert-advice/papers/yr2013/languages-in-aotearoa-new-zealand/

Endnotes

1   Cook Islands Māori.

Chapter 7 Multilingual children, monolingual teachers: Mangere Bridge Kindergarten

Carol Hartley, Pat Rogers, Jemma Smith and Daniel Lovatt; with Nola Harvey and Helen Hedges

He moana pukepuke e ekengia e te waka.
A choppy sea can be navigated (persevere during turbulent waters).

Introduction

Mangere Bridge Kindergarten was built in 1975 and operates under the governance of the Auckland Kindergarten Association. It is sited within a residential area and has a long history of community involvement. Located on a peninsula in South Auckland, the kindergarten community highly values the areas of local significance: Ambury Regional Farm Park and Mangere Mountain.

The kindergarten is an English-medium centre, and the operating model changed in 2013 from a sessional kindergarten to a day-model kindergarten (8:30 am to 2:30 pm). As a result of this change the permanent teaching team increased from three to four teachers to comply with a 1:10 teacher:child ratio. The permanent teaching team are all fully qualified, registered teachers with three holding postgraduate qualifications. The number of families belonging to the kindergarten fluctuates between 55 and 60, with a maximum of 40 children on the roll on any one day.

The Mangere Bridge community is diverse: culturally, linguistically, ethnically and economically. The kindergarten community comprises a demographic mix of approximately 48 percent Pākehā, 17 percent Māori, 17 percent Pasifika, and 10 percent Asian or South-East Asian, with the remainder made up of people identifying with a range of ethnicities, from Africa, Australia, the United States of America, Europe and the United Kingdom.

The kindergarten's philosophy statement highlights a fundamental belief in the importance of working to forge partnerships between teachers, children, families and the community. Also fundamental to the joint philosophy of the teaching team is the non-negotiable nature of an inclusive environment, one that recognises children as individuals with their own strengths and funds of knowledge (González, Moll, & Amanti, 2005). The value of play to support children's learning is embedded in practice. Teachers provide an environment that is safe, challenging and stimulating, and where responsibility for self and others is valued.

Participants in the research

Teachers

Seven teachers completed teacher questionnaires and participated in the teacher focus group (the four permanent full-time teachers, one long-term reliever and two student teachers). Four of these participants had backgrounds that included languages other than English; however, all of the permanent teachers considered themselves monolingual English speakers. These four all live in the Mangere Bridge community, are long-time residents, and the community's history and stories are an integral part of their own life stories.

Parents

In total, 38 parents completed questionnaires. Teachers selected the focus group parents to gain input from as wide a representation as possible of the diversity of languages within the centre. Criteria included families with a variety of languages, cultures and ethnicities; families where the adults spoke different languages from one another; families with intergenerational diversity; and a mixture of long-term Aotearoa New Zealand residents and new arrivals. All participants chosen were comfortable to communicate in the English language. Ten adults from the Mangere Bridge community participated in the parent and whānau focus group, including two couples and one mother/daughter pair (i.e. seven families were represented). These adults represented 15 different languages.

Children

Ten children agreed to be interviewed. There were eight individual interviews and one sibling interview, conducted with the two children together.

Findings

Research Question 1: What languages do children from participating ECE centres use in their learning in the centre and at home?

The parent questionnaire indicated that there were 26 languages spoken among the kindergarten community, with some children confidently speaking three or more languages in their homes and community. Parents stated clearly that they worked hard to sustain home languages. For example a parent who makes use of four languages said that

> I've got some friends who understand both … [and] regret not learning their roots and their own language … as children they decided not to listen, to stick to the, to English as their language and their parents didn't push the issue, but now as adults they're regretting not having decided to learn their language … so for that reason I kind of would like to keep pushing the issue with the children even if they don't want to reply in English or in French or Vietnamese, I still will try to keep talking to them in those languages because I don't want them to grow up and feel like they have missed out. (Parent 5, focus group)

Another parent took a more formal approach to reinforce his point that "a little is not enough":

I teach them at home [for] nearly three and a half years … I teach them reading and writing … they speak [with] fluency in my first language. Between themselves they speak English [as it] is easier but with us [it is a] hundred per cent speaking [the heritage/home language]. (Parent 7, focus group)

Figure 7.1: Multilingual greetings displayed at Mangere Bridge Kindergarten

Families noted that the challenges were even more pronounced when there was only one parent who was bilingual. For example, one parent shared that it was hard to keep her language:

My husband speaking English and then my children are like, 'He doesn't' [speak mum's language]. Maybe [my child can] understand [my language] a little bit but when Daddy's there, he thought, oh it's better, you know, to talk English. (Parent 4, focus group)

Another parent pointed out that families have serious responsibilities with regard to language maintenance: "If somebody is not very careful or doesn't care much which language the children learn, within [the] first generation [they] change to English." (Parent 7, focus group)

The kindergarten included several families who work transnationally. Grandparents reported their own rich language repertoire as they followed their children to several countries in order to support their grandchildren. They recounted that they learned a new language each time in the new host country. They had taken on this responsibility in the belief that this would support their grandchildren in their education.

In the centre, teachers speak English. The children communicate in English and on occasion in their own heritage/home language during play. In the focus group, teachers reported that some children who shared a heritage/home language in common, for example Tongan or German, often communicated using both their heritage/home language and English. During mat times the children used English to interact, talk and respond. At arrival and departure times, observations showed that parents regularly used their heritage/home language with their children and code switched between heritage/home language and English. Some of the many heritage/home languages recorded at these times were Japanese, Karen, French, Basque, Dutch, Vietnamese, Kurdish, Gujarati, Hindi, Māori, Samoan and Tongan.

Parents reported that in the home, children use both their heritage/home language/s and English. However, there were reports from parents that some children who had been using their heritage/home language regularly for the majority of the time began using English more in the home once they were settled at kindergarten.

Research Question 2: What experiences and outcomes for children who learn in more than one language in the early years are valued by parents, teachers and children?

The analyses of the teacher and parent focus group interviews and the questionnaire data showed considerable consistency in terms of valued experiences and outcomes. The overarching themes from the teachers' focus group include a strong emphasis on the importance of relationships and inclusive practice. Teachers expressed ideas consistent with an additive approach to languages and literacies (Cummins, 2009; Taylor, Bernhard, Garg, & Cummins, 2008), valuing the support of parents to introduce home languages into the kindergarten, and building partnerships with parents to foster children's sense of belonging and multiple identities.

Teachers' values and actions were formed by experience and driven by professional knowledge and understandings of the New Zealand curriculum *Te Whāriki* (Ministry of Education, 1996). Teachers valued the importance of retaining the child's home languages and cultures, and understood and acknowledged how parents valued their heritage/home languages. Teachers recognised, however, that it was not feasible to 'teach' 26 languages within the kindergarten.

This viewpoint was also evident in the experiences valued by parents, many of whom were emphatic that the responsibility for maintaining the heritage/home language sat within the home. One parent echoed the majority views of the group: "This is what I think. It is my responsibility." (Parent 7, focus group).

Focus group parents' and teachers' comments on the children's experiences, and the learning outcomes they valued, formed three key themes:

1. relationships
2. identities
3. environments and communities.

1. Relationships

Teachers referred often to the importance of knowing children and families well. Developing relationships and family and community are both foundational principles of *Te Whāriki* (Ministry of Education, 1996). Teachers considered children's learning outcomes depended on the teachers' knowledge of each child, and that a child's sense of belonging depended on their ability to engage with peers and adults in their lives. This engagement was in their home language in the extended family and whānau, most often with grandparents, and in English in the kindergarten environment.

Several parents spoke of the value of the heritage/home languages in maintaining intergenerational relationships. For example, one parent commented, "We speak [our home language] a lot to the children because their grandparents and great-grandparents are still around …" (Parent 2, focus group). Another commented, "My mum, she said, 'Please teach your children [our language] so I can communicate with them'" (Parent 4, focus group).

Parents' comments endorsed the centre practices that reflected the principle of additive bilingualism. The parents valued the play-based curriculum as they saw their children acquiring English during their experiences with other children in the centre. They stated that they had enrolled their child in an English-medium centre in order for their child to *add* English language to their heritage/home language. An additive bilingual approach was consistent with the beliefs and philosophy of the teachers, who expressed a desire to work inclusively with children's heritage/home languages and cultures to foster strong responsive and reciprocal relationships in the kindergarten environment.

However differing views within families, reflected within society as a whole, presented challenges (McCaffery & McFall-McCaffery, 2010; Royal Society of New Zealand, 2013). Often families were unsure what might be best for their children. One parent in a household may have wanted the child to attend a language immersion or bilingual centre, whereas the other parent was clear that English was the priority language for education in Aotearoa New Zealand.

> I come from a big family… At home we speak some Tongan and English to my son … We came here [in] 2006 … We try to learn English but … my husband wanted my son to go attend …Tongan … school … I want him to get a better education in the future. I just want to take my son, our son … to the English kindergarten … Yeah I want him to speak the language [English] [and] our own language. (Parent 3, focus group)

2. Identities

Members of the parent and whānau focus group stated emphatically that identity is inextricably tied to language. For example, one parent commented, "I think cultural identity is a responsibility of parents and language is cultural identity." (Parent 6, focus group)

Parents drew on their own experiences and funds of knowledge in understanding the link between language and identity and were aware of the complexities of retaining their own heritage/home language in an English-dominant culture. They valued English for the opportunities and status it would give their children for education and employment in the global arena. Parents also had aspirations for their children to be able to return to their home country and to speak the language of that country, including being able to gain financially and personally rewarding employment in that country.

> I plan to send them back every 2, 3 years. They stay there for 2, 3 months, 4 months, to rebuild their first language [before] coming

> back here... So hopefully if one day they change their mind to go back to our country it is easier for them to [get a] job with the first language. So this is my plan. (Parent 7, focus group)

A valued outcome was to be both a global citizen *and* a local citizen; one who works in multiple worlds, able to communicate competently in the language of the country their children are in at the time.

However, a parent born in Europe recounted in his story a caution that illustrated concerns about loss of identity and language that several others confirmed:

> My family emigrated here when I was five ... I try to speak [my home language] to them, [the children] most of the time but because I was five, my vocabulary's kind of plateaued, just a little bit above five, [for] more advanced financial concepts and so forth I prefer English ... I tend to speak [my home language] with my mother and she looks after the children a lot and speaks [it] with them as well. (Parent 6, focus group)

3. Environments and communities

Children from the kindergarten experience a variety of environments and communities in their everyday lives. A third of the parents who completed the questionnaire reported a desire for their children to "fit in" to the range of environments and diverse communities that their children move between in Aotearoa New Zealand. They wanted their children to be able to engage with the *social community* of sports, neighbours and other places; the *educational community* of kindergarten, school and later tertiary study; and the *heritage community* of home, wider family, church and homeland.

In the social community several noted that their children developed friendships in these groups and with their neighbours where English was the language for everyday interactions. "Cos their friends come from different cultures and they're not Samoan, so they speak English." (Parent 1, focus group)

Parents recognised the value of bilingualism for cognitive development. One parent commented, "[Being bilingual] also helps with maths, like with Japanese [it] teaches numbers differently ... It will allow their brain to wire a little bit differently" (Parent 6, focus group). However, parents also expressed uncertainty about how this priority aligned with those of the wider educational community. They also saw challenges ahead for children and family members to grow the capacity to achieve the level of language competencies needed to continue their academic learning in more than one language. Parents also showed concern for their children's competencies in English to meet current monolingual school expectations.

Each parent considered heritage/home languages valuable for maintaining identities and contact with the child's cultures and heritages. Every parent strongly endorsed the value of using the heritage/home language for their child to sustain relationships with grandparents and the wider family. Each had a story to tell about how they treasured their heritage/home language particularly for this purpose. Parents recounted telling stories to their children of their childhood in heritage/home languages in the evenings as a regular practice to bring to life their home country and cultures.

> They're becoming quite fascinated as to what my childhood was like … then I tried to help them visualise where that was taking place at my home [country]. (Parent 2, focus group)

Others talked of locating and making good use of DVDs, YouTube clips and other digital resources to nurture the heritage/home language.

A parent reported discussing with her husband whether they should have their child in the *palagi* (English) or Tongan speaking group of their church:

> I want him to go to the Tongan ward [group] so he can learn the Tongan … I just want my son since he is growing up in New Zealand to know more about my culture and the language … I don't want him to lose the language. (Parent 3, focus group)

The multiple worlds and communities children inhabit create both challenges and opportunities. Responses from the parent focus group and questionnaire identified a major challenge as ensuring their children are happy and able to fit into the diverse communities to which their children now belong. Parents found it increasingly difficult to maintain their heritage/home languages as the child's social connections with English speakers increased. This leads to consideration of research question 3.

Research question 3: How might the opportunities and challenges for children who learn in more than one language be addressed in educational practice?

Findings for this question revealed how complex the issue of language usage and learning is in English-medium settings. This complexity resulted in challenges for teachers as parents' comments provoked reflection and changes to their existing practices.

The key themes in the findings suggested there are many opportunities and challenges for children and teachers in educational practices that were identified by teachers and parents. Themes from the teachers' focus group emphasised the importance of opportunities related to inclusive practice, community and relationships, a strengths-based curriculum, and formative assessment as a means of knowing children and families and to support a sense of belonging. However, a major challenge in this context was to adequately acknowledge and include the languages present in such a diverse kindergarten community.

The findings highlighted that both parents and teachers see being bilingual and/or multilingual as a major opportunity for children, cognitively, educationally and socially, while also presenting challenges. Using an inclusive lens, teachers viewed challenges and opportunities as mutually reciprocal. Having 26 different heritage/home languages in the kindergarten could be seen as a challenge for children, and perhaps an insurmountable challenge for teachers to address while simultaneously providing a strong grounding in English. However, in keeping with Mangere Bridge Kindergarten's inclusive philosophy, teachers approached this challenge as an opportunity. They sought to explore and locate meaningful ways to respectfully respond to, and support, all of the children and their whānau. This section presents some possibilities in terms of responses developed during the research to address the opportunities and challenges of multiple home languages in this context. It also highlights further areas for teacher consideration.

The teachers redrafted the philosophy statement to include a statement on languages after participating in the first meeting of the project's advisory/reference group, where advisers and experts identified this as a priority for centres and schools. During the process of the research, teachers also changed the children's portfolios by including spaces inside and on the cover to prioritise the child and his/her family's language and cultural identities. Teachers reported that the new portfolios became a point of deeper connection with families: many expressed appreciation of the opportunity to reawaken cultural and languages histories. Teachers from the new entrant classes at two neighbouring schools requested that the languages and cultural information be included in the kindergarten's transition-to-school portfolios to provide a valuable introduction to the child and family. Teachers documented children's fascination with language differences and noted that inquiries about languages spoken, generated initially from the use of individualised language greetings at mat time, became part of home conversations too.

The teaching team made time to discuss, reflect on, critique and search for opportunities in amongst the challenges. This occurred through informal discussions throughout the day and some regular in-depth dialogue occasions once children had left at the end of the day. The research highlighted the challenges and rich opportunities that a bi/multilingual context provided, enabling the construct of children who learn in more than one language to be foregrounded in thinking, planning, and pedagogy. Team discussions promoted the idea of incremental rather than wholesale changes as the teachers planned respectfully to support all children and their whānau. These incremental changes could be seen as taking an additive approach in teaching responses, continuing to value the existing kindergarten culture and environment but adding further richness and complexity. The ways in which teachers responded to and supported children's multiple heritage/home languages and English, and continued to honour tangata whenua, are outlined here.

The teaching team already had a strong custom of bringing a story of the local community (the Hape story), related to the legend of Mangere mountain (Te Pane o Mataoho), to the children and families as part of everyday practices. The team made use of aspects of te reo Māori and tikanga Māori in the form of storytelling and waiata. Mat time is a daily experience where all children and teachers come together in one large group to sing, dance, play, read and share. Teachers see mat time as a time of relationship building, identity building and empowerment for the children, and it seemed an obvious place to affirm the many heritage/home languages. Teachers began to reflect on how they could uphold, support and promote children's heritage/home languages through mat times in order to further meet their inclusive philosophy.

Using the previous experience of a community/mat time at the beginning of each day, and the familiar routine of learning the days of the week in te reo Māori, teachers began by working with parents and whānau to create visual prompt cards of days of the week in each of the children's heritage/home languages. Parents willingly supplied the scripts, each of which was printed in a different colour and laminated. Parents also provided valuable pronunciation guides, recorded on the back of cards for quick teacher reference.

Teachers made use of the cards in different ways at mat times. Through their regular use children quickly understood that these were meaningful words, and that they represented different languages and scripts. Children recognised and identified with what the cards represented, knowing that each card represented a language; some also recognised immediately the colour of the script in which their heritage/home language was written, and often those of their friends too. When interviewed and asked which language her Dad used in order to speak to her, a child quickly replied, "You know … it's the green one".

Teachers often referred to the pronunciation guide on the back of the cards and sought the children's help, showing that teachers were learners too. Mat times provided an opportunity to respectfully support heritage/home languages, viewing children and families and whānau as experts and teachers as learners. The balance of power often shifted through this acknowledgement of each child's identity. A powerful spin-off was that a renewed sense of belonging and empowerment appeared in the kindergarten community.

The success of using these artefacts each day at mat time, and the early conversations about languages, provoked teachers to reflect on other ways children, family and whānau might be welcomed and acknowledged. Prior to the research, teachers already sang greetings to children as individuals and as a group used Māori and some Pasifika greetings consistently. The decision to add each of the children's heritage/home language greetings to their repertoire emerged from the reflective discussions. Teachers asked parents for an appropriate greeting from their heritage/home language to use at kindergarten. With their support these were also added to mat time welcome songs.

The use of these resources at mat times provoked much discussion and questioning. As teachers explored this new learning together, the children's initial responses surprised them. For example, when teachers asked the children which languages they spoke, or how they said hello at home, they were often puzzled. Teachers began to see that many of the children who spoke more than one language and very capably switched between languages (in some cases three or four languages) when they spoke to different people, did so instinctively. The children for whom English was their only language were similarly unaware that the language they were speaking also had a name and was a valid language, often saying something like "I don't have one of those". Children did not appear to identify with the names of the languages.

"I just speak normal"

A defining moment for the teachers occurred when one of the children responded to a question about what language she spoke. She shook her head and said, "I don't have one of those … I just speak normal". It was at that point teachers realised they had not been naming or making distinctions between the languages.

Teachers documented that children's identities changed as they took on this view of themselves and their friends as not only speakers of a language or languages, but also as individuals with a culture or cultures that were recognised and valued positively. The cards supported children to recognise their own language among other text. When revisiting his portfolio on one occasion, a child commented, "Hey look that's my other language, my second language."

This heightened metalinguistic awareness appeared to add complexity to children's understanding of difference. Teachers noticed that some children more than willingly took on others' identities and used different languages and cultures to make links with other children and form groups. A South African / New Zealand child would often ask to be greeted in Tongan, as he associated with his Tongan friends and used language as a tool to belong to their group. It was not unusual for this group of boys to demonstrate their shared Aotearoa New Zealand identity and perform their understanding of a Māori haka. The children became fluent in other language greetings and began to explore a range of possible identities. Teachers became comfortable with these playful shifts in identity. This recognition of languages and identities spilled over into children's other communities and home experiences. After a holiday break, a parent shared with great delight that a child enquired as they passed through each small Aotearoa New Zealand town, "What language do they speak here?"

Implementing changes to mat times through using children's heritage/home languages was just the beginning of easing the challenges facing children. Teachers next reflected upon another valuable artefact central to belonging in the kindergarten: children's portfolios. Portfolios, containing learning stories (Carr, 2001) as documentation of children's learning, had long been used to build a relationship and a sense of belonging, and as a way for children to connect experiences at kindergarten, at home, and in their other life worlds and communities. Teachers pondered, "How can we better reflect the children's home languages and cultures in their portfolios?" Because of the role the portfolio plays as a carrier of identity from home to kindergarten to school (Hartley, Rogers, Smith, Peters, & Carr, 2012), teachers considered some incremental changes in order to retain their structure and familiarity while attempting to add further value. Teachers worked to find central ways to represent the child's home cultures and identities in their kindergarten portfolio in order to provide meaningful and recognisable connections for these children.

When new children started attending the kindergarten, teachers talked with each child and their family about the cultures they identified with and then worked together to reflect this on the cover of their portfolio. The portfolio covers provided a simple way for families to make connections between their home and the kindergarten and opened up opportunities early in their kindergarten/educational journey for rich discussion about culture and language.

One of the first new cover pages was for a child whose mother was Indonesian. In consultation with the mother, a batik fabric pattern was added as a border. Upon seeing this for the first time, it was greeted with considerable emotion by the mother, who felt this was a highly respectful way to honour her family culture and language in the kindergarten.

Figure 7.2: Portfolio covers for the four teachers at Mangere Bridge Kindergarten

The first few portfolio covers were largely teacher led, but this has changed over time as the process became embedded in the kindergarten culture. Teachers recognised that parents have deep funds of knowledge about their heritage, and in asking for their input viewed this as a way to empower families and whānau to make decisions about their child's covers. This might involve choosing from examples of other children's portfolios displayed in the kindergarten, emailing a picture that is meaningful to them, or suggesting a unique cover worked on together. The action of adding a culturally representative cover, implemented in a respectful way, created an empowering place for dialogue between children, teachers and whānau, and within families.

The request to families for input into the cover design also provoked some new families to think more deeply about their heritage. From an initial comment such as, "Oh we are just Kiwis", families later reported further thinking and a deeper awareness of cultural influences in their families they were willing to share.

The success with how the individual portfolio covers reflected children's family identities, languages and cultures prompted teachers to reflect critically on ways to represent these further in children's portfolios and in the wider kindergarten environment. Teachers now write a story of the children's first day at kindergarten to reflect their portfolio cover and welcome them using the appropriate languages and script. The photos of children displayed in the teaching and learning environment are also bordered to match their portfolios.

Relationships with families have deepened as teachers have learned more about each other and made connections that have originated through rich conversations started around creating children's portfolios together. Moreover, as teachers have worked with families to design their child's portfolio and offered choices about decisions for the cover, they have experienced in practice that identity is complex, and that as teachers they cannot make assumptions about how families view themselves. Due to the diversity of families and complex cultural dynamics, tensions might arise if teachers attempted to fix an identity. Some families chose up to four different patterns or images for the cover to signal rich and mixed languages and cultural heritages, whereas other families with mixed languages and cultural heritages chose to identify as New Zealanders first and foremost—an iconic kiwi border and/or a silver fern became popular cover images.

Teachers wondered if the cultural images and backgrounds would foster recognition of a shared linguistic and cultural heritage between children as they identified with other children with similar covers. We noticed that children looking through portfolios recognised similar covers and patterns to their own, and that this created different connection points and additional pathways for belonging.

Conclusion

Teachers viewed the research as a stimulus to deepen everyday conversations about languages and cultural heritages with families. The research became an opportunity to appreciate the richness of the community languages and the efforts parents were prepared to make to maintain their heritage/home languages. It also became an opportunity to work in tandem/partnership with families to complement their efforts. The authentic relationships with families already established provided the fertile ground for sharing their aspirations and values for their children, and later, ways their languages and cultures could be included more in the kindergarten.

Teachers realised more strongly than previously that they had a responsibility and a part to play in the children's future as bilingual or multilingual members of society. As a result, they continued to explore the development of pedagogical strategies, artefacts and resources to strengthen and promote the heritage/home languages within the kindergarten community. The children were open to sharing their languages and became enthusiastic 'researchers' about language themselves.

It was daunting for this team of monolingual teachers to recognise more deeply that the kindergarten community had such a diversity of languages and to grapple with the associated pedagogical challenges and opportunities. Teachers realised there was no quick fix nor a formula. A myriad of challenges and opportunities were embraced, and rather than become overwhelmed, teachers began with the known, familiar practices that children were already comfortable with, then set about to learn more, to research, read and engage in reflection and dialogue among the team. Exploration and responses have been developed over time through responding constantly to the changing dynamics of kindergarten families. Promoting multiple languages became and remains a pedagogical focus for the team.

One parent voiced a common aspiration from both the questionnaire and the focus group findings that is pertinent to the entire project: "Our kids are our future and I know that we all want the best for our children. We want them to succeed and do better than we did" (Parent 1, focus group).

References

Carr, M. (2001). *Assessment in early childhood settings: Learning stories.* London, UK: Paul Chapman.

Cummins, J. (2009). Pedagogies of choice: Challenging coercive relations of power in classrooms and communities. *International Journal of Bilingual Education and Bilingualism, 12*(30), 261–271. doi: 10.1080/136700509/03003751

González, N., Moll, L. C., & Amanti, C. (2005). *Funds of knowledge: Theorizing practices in households, communities and classrooms.* Mahwah, NJ: Erlbaum.

Hartley, C., Rogers, P., Smith, J., Peters, S., & Carr, M. (2012). *Crossing the border: A community negotiates the transition from early childhood to primary school.* Wellington: NZCER Press.

McCaffery, J., & McFall-McCaffery, J. (2010). O tatatou o agaʻi i fea? / ʻOku tatu o ki fe? / Where are we heading?: Pacific languages in Aotearoa / New Zealand. *AlterNative Special Supplement Issue Ngaahi Lea ʻa e Kakai Pasifiki: Endangered Pacific Languages and Cultures, 6*(2), 86–121.

Ministry of Education. (1996). *Te whāriki: He whāriki mātauranga mō ngā mokopuna o Aotearoa: Early childhood curriculum*. Wellington: Learning Media. Retrieved from http://www.education.govt.nz/early-childhood/teaching-and-learning/ece-curriculum/

Royal Society of New Zealand. (2013). *Languages in Aotearoa New Zealand*. Wellington: Author. Retrieved from http://www.royalsociety.org.nz/expert-advice/papers/yr2013/languages-in-aotearoa-new-zealand/

Taylor, L. K., Bernhard, J. K., Garg, S., & Cummins, J. (2008). Affirming plural belonging: Building on students' family-based cultural and linguistic capital through multiliteracies pedagogy. *Journal of Early Childhood Literacy, 8*(3), 269–294. doi: 10.1177/1468798408096481

Chapter 8 Conclusions: Insightful landings

Nola Harvey, Helen Hedges, Valerie N. Podmore and Peter J. Keegan

> *He pukepuke maunga e pikitia e te tangata,*
> *he pukepuke moana e ekea e te waka.*
> *A steep mountain can be climbed by a person;*
> *a steep sea can be ridden by a canoe.*

Introduction

This final whakataukī, an extension of the whakataukī in Chapter 1, suggests that our team of researchers and teachers surmounted various challenges in order to gain some valuable new insights from this study. The study provided an opportunity to acknowledge, recognise and enhance, share concerns and misapprehensions, and explore the value of learning in and through more than one language in early childhood settings. The findings also supported the value of immersion practices to revitalise or maintain indigenous language/s.

During this study, teacher-researchers reported growing confidence, knowledge and actions in relation to partnerships with bi- and multi-lingual families. The research became a catalyst for changes, as follows:

- children settling other children who spoke similar languages
- language being used as a cognitive resource, not just a settling resource
- languages becoming a way for children and families to connect more
- teachers extending the range of languages used beyond greetings and simple words to include stories in diverse languages
- the whole community becoming a wider resource
- reciprocal and extended relationships growing within the centre whānau and community.

The overall findings within and across the four centres, together with the teacher-researchers' concluding reflections, illustrated how the centres were all different, changing and dynamic with regard to the use of languages. There were different implications for practice, as indicated by the teachers' reflections in each centre chapter. Related to these implications, the findings across the four centre settings indicated that the ethos and culture of the centre were important in creating an empowering environment supporting an additive approach to bilingualism for learning and teaching. Where parents or teachers did not already have the resources, they were able to draw on the language resources embedded in the funds of knowledge within their communities, including parents, community elders and the children.

Further, across the four centres' learning and teaching contexts, this research showed strong and powerful images of children as they built their identities and language resources. At all four centres, te reo Māori was evident and being encouraged, perhaps influenced by professional uptake of *Te Whāriki* and greater use of te reo Māori in teacher education. Teachers at all four centres reported some knowledge of te reo Māori. Parents, other than those at the Māori-medium centre (Te Puna Kōhungahunga), reported knowledge of te reo Māori. Observer XT analyses demonstrated the use of te reo Māori during group sessions at both English-medium centres (Mangere Bridge Kindergarten and Symonds Street Early Childhood Centre). While the extent to which such practices are widespread in other centres is as yet unknown, it was encouraging to find Māori being used outside of Māori-medium ECE centres, especially given the well-known slow decline in Māori-medium

ECE numbers over the last decade, the census findings showing a continuing decrease in te reo Māori, and the long-held concerns of Ritchie (2008, 2013).

Each centre was distinctive in nature, whether Samoan immersion, Māori-medium or English-medium. The findings, and the subsequent changes made in the centres' teaching practices and approaches prompted by the research project, showed how multiple languages can be fostered intentionally in planned and systematic ways by teachers who are fluently bilingual, multilingual or, in one setting, monolingual. One implication for teacher education and policy, then, is that teachers need the professional knowledge, skills, attitudes and pedagogical understanding to enact additive bilingual approaches and practices, and to engage with the local funds of knowledge within the centres and local communities.

This chapter provides further syntheses of findings across four ECE centres, with reference to the concept of mana and with a particular focus on the principles and strands of *Te Whāriki*, the New Zealand early childhood curriculum (Ministry of Education, 1996). There is also a discussion of implications for teaching, research and theory.

The significance of mana

The opening whakataukī in the preface of this book refers to the concept of *mana*. Moreover 'mana' is a word used prominently in *Te Whāriki*. It is a concept in Aotearoa New Zealand with a wide variety of meanings; for example, "prestige, authority, control, power, influence, status, spiritual power, charisma, jurisdiction, mandate, freedom" (Moorfield, 2011, p. 94–95). Reedy (2013) used this concept to describe critical ways teachers must ensure that children are empowered to achieve their potential and have control of their learning and destinies. *Empowerment* is one principle in *Te Whāriki*. Reedy also indicates that the other three principles of *Te Whāriki* (*relationships, family and community* and *holistic development*) are embedded in the concept of mana.

Five examples of mana are included as the strands of *Te Whāriki*. Reedy's chapter outlines the following. Mana atua links with the strand of wellbeing and recognises the uniqueness of each child that ought to be nurtured and celebrated. Mana tangata links with the strand of contribution, upholding the importance of reciprocity and mutual support in relationships, and the ability to develop physical and emotional skills and connectedness. Mana reo is the strand of communication, where fluency in languages empowers children and develops cultural understanding. Mana whenua is the strand of belonging, where identities are highlighted. Mana aotūroa is about curiosity and a quest for knowledge, and therefore links to exploration. The next section summarises findings across the four diverse ECE centres that connected strongly to the principles and strands of *Te Whāriki*.

Principles of Te Whāriki

The principles of *relationships, family and community* and *holistic development* were clearly evident in the findings, and it was clear that the principle of *empowerment* guided the philosophy and practices of each centre. However, the findings also showed that each centre had its own priorities and pedagogical pathways. These priorities and pathways were consistent with and reflected the communities and contexts that each centre served, and were embedded in specific valued language/s and educational aspirations. Consistent with the aspiration statement in *Te Whāriki*, parents and teachers valued fostering children as competent, confident learners and communicators who were strong in their identities through engaging with their languages and cultures. The following indicates the ways in which the principles were evident in the findings.

Empowerment—whakamana

The questionnaire findings provided in-depth knowledge about children's languages spoken at home. In addition, many teachers discovered the wealth of heritage/home languages available in each teaching team. Realising this richness in the centre and community enabled teachers to more overtly draw on everyone's language resources. As a consequence, teachers and children were recognised as competent and confident communicators, each individual able to confidently bring their kete (basket) of language and cultural resources to the educational setting. Both monolingual and bi/multilingual children were viewed as identity-rich communicators, ready to engage cognitively through their non-verbal and verbal languages (Cummins, 2009; Kenner, Gregory, Ruby, & Al-Azami, 2008).

This interest in and attention to children's identities and languages stimulated critical reflection among teachers about the value placed on these things in the centres' philosophies and practices. Some teachers asked themselves questions such as: How are we enacting inclusion? In what ways are we protecting and promoting children's access to their heritage/home languages and working in children's best interests for successful participation? How might we communicate to families that we know that their child's language and cultural resources (i.e. funds of knowledge) are recognised as valuable for learning in the centre? What funds of knowledge have we activated within the teaching team? The study enabled professional opportunities for teachers to shift gaps or deficit views about the value of languages for learning, particularly in the English-medium settings, that were identified in the questionnaire and focus group findings.

Relationships—ngā hononga
Through documenting family languages, aspirations and teaching practices, teachers shifted their views of the place all languages can play in learning. By encouraging family contributions, and working intentionally to make purposeful use of every communicative tool within everyday interactions, teachers could build on both non-verbal and home-language phrases to build trusting and stimulating relationships. For example, teachers drawing on colleagues and family members were able to build up repertoires of vocabulary, non-verbal and visual language processes and strategies to enhance children's expressive language capacities and conceptual transfer during learning and teaching. These actions became a basis to build relationships that went beyond symbolic efforts with languages other than the medium of instruction to enact more respectful and reciprocal relationships. Deeper engagements resulted that opened up opportunities for the rich use of languages as learning resources for all children.

All four centres already had well-established home–centre relationships. Within the English-medium settings, documenting for and talking with families about the wealth of languages and working collaboratively to strengthen relationships caused a reconsideration of the portfolios at Mangere Bridge Kindergarten and the possible language and cultural contributions at Symonds Street Early Childhood Centre. Beyond the questionnaires, teachers were empowered to strengthen relationships and understanding through deeper evaluative processes provoked by the focus group conversations. These exchanges prompted a more overt and holistic valuing of the range of languages represented in each centre community beyond the language of instruction.

Family and community—whānau tangata

Empowering learners begins with respecting each child as a member of a family and community. The questionnaire findings, and subsequent conversations about languages that developed, enabled teachers to know better each family's languages and cultural practices. These conversations became a pathway for exploring aspirations and concerns for each child's educational development and desired futures. Families wanted their children to enjoy diversity, be included respectfully in educational settings, and find their place in Aotearoa New Zealand. Hence, people, places and things of value to families became legitimate conversation topics. Teachers recognised the passion and enduring pride families have for their cultural and spiritual heritages, languages and expressive arts, and plural identities.

Teacher-researchers were then open to following up opportunities for including families' languages, literacies and funds of knowledge. Families felt empowered to bring in their community stories and cultural tools at any time, not just for specific, time-bound celebrations, and not dependent on the medium of instruction in the particular centre. Further, there were opportunities for teachers to make effective use of a range of literature with all children. This was particularly important for children taking on a heritage language, perhaps not spoken at home, where there may be limited opportunities to see printed material in the heritage language. Reading aloud in English, te reo Māori or Samoan strengthened overall experiences with oral and written language. Even when children do not understand a language, they are experiencing the way books work, print conventions, and visual language layout and design; in other words, metalinguistic activities that lay the foundation for later reading, writing, bi/multiliteracies and identity texts (Cummins, 2009; Kenner & Kress, 2003).

Holistic development—kotahitanga

The process and findings of the questionnaires and parent/whānau focus groups, and subsequent conversations about families' languages and cultural practices, became a pathway for exploring aspirations and concerns for each child's social, spiritual, affective and educational development and desired futures. Viewing the child as "with languages" rather than "without language" respects the learning and funds of knowledge the child is building and using at home in a bilingual household. The rich and collaborative curriculum experiences that resulted (e.g. the Indonesian angklung experience at Symonds Street Early Childhood Centre) appeared to deepen respect for diversity among children and encouraged questions and exploration about languages and cultures that linked physical, cognitive, emotional and spiritual development.

Strands of Te Whāriki

Findings from all four centres included themes that were related to the strands of *Te Whāriki*; for example: Whanaungatanga / Family and community, Holistic development, and Belonging. When children were recognised and respected for who they are, and their languages and cultures had status and currency in the centre environment (Cummins, 2009; Garcia & Wei, 2014), the strands were woven strongly. Examples presented below highlight particular strands.

Wellbeing—mana atua

The nature of the Samoan-language immersion environment at the A'oga Fa'a Samoa, together with the familiar artefacts and *fale* setting, created a sense of trust. Attention to the protocols such as *lotu*, and accepting the spiritual life of the child and family, served as a familiar anchor and for relational engagement among teachers and family members alike. Sensitivity to the cultural and spiritual needs of the very youngest and oldest child were also embedded in the close attention to whanaungatanga and wairua tanga that tamariki experienced on the whāriki at Te Puna Kōhungahunga. The words and rhythms of the mihi and pepeha generated a secure sense of wellbeing, and of place and identity.

Teachers initiated trusting relationships at Mangere Bridge Kindergarten through significant attention to each family's cultures, languages and heritages during enrolment processes. Opportunity for parents or a whānau member to make a personal choice about the detail and representation of their child's multiple identities enabled family members to understand that teachers were committed to supporting heritage/home languages and an inclusive culture in the centre community. Categorisations and assumptions, common in monolingual settings, were avoided. The use of in-depth conversations and inclusive artefacts such as the Global Whānau Board at the Symonds Street Early Childhood Centre generated daily opportunities for bi/multilingual teachers to model and discuss languages and cultures directly with family and whānau. As trust built between the adults, children new to Aotearoa New Zealand and the English-medium setting could recognise the non-verbal 'social' affirmations of their family members and begin to see that the centre was a place of security and acceptance of languages. Sensitivity to settling a child through use of their heritage/home language became paramount.

Belonging—mana whenua

Children at Te Puna Kōhungahunga and the A'oga Fa'a Samoa had a strong sense of belonging created through daily acknowledgement and use of their heritage/home language of te reo Māori or Samoan, respectively. Personalised affirmations were embedded in language protocols and routines. Familiar phrases, stories and objects of interest from home help to settle children. An exchange of cultural resources and language-rich artefacts and literature prompted by the research led to deeper feelings of belonging and wellbeing, enabling children to feel included and part of the Symonds Street Early Childhood Centre community. Sharing a home language with a teacher ensured a child's interests and abilities were recognised and acted upon. At Mangere Bridge Kindergarten this development included creating a stronger presence in their portfolios for children's rich heritages and identities, and major changes to mat time welcome routines through the use of children's heritage/home oral and written language greetings.

Contribution—mana tangata

Increasing use of heritage/home languages in centres became open invitations to family and whānau to offer greater contributions that, in turn, enhanced children's connections with people, places and things. For example, children in the A'oga Fa'a Samoa and Te Puna Kōhungahunga were already using the traditional language structures and phrases from earlier generations for protocols during special occasions, as they applied what they had learned as part of their *lotu* and pepeha. The power of positive use of the Samoan language was noted particularly by family members, and they expressed pride in the way their children could use Samoan for their learning. Some parents recognised the value of the confident child bringing Samoan into regular use at home—reversing the language shift between generations that had occurred in their childhood.

The enactment of tuakana–teina was evident not only in Te Puna Kōhungahunga but also at Symonds Street Early Childhood Centre, where an older child showed confident use of their heritage/home language as a resource for contributing support for a younger child in settling into the new English-medium environment. Children and teachers encouraged a confident Japanese-speaking grandmother to share finger rhymes and songs in Japanese, with her grandson's able assistance, and many children took up the opportunity as willing listeners and responders to impromptu readings in home languages of favourite picture books or enactments of familiar stories.

Communication—mana reo

At Te Puna Kōhungahunga and the A'oga Fa'a Samoa, heritage/home languages were already established as taonga and were used purposefully and systematically for education and care. For example, whether supporting pōwhiri occasions at Tūtahi Tonu marae or in their visits to other whānau members' marae, children gained opportunities as tangata whenua (hosts) or manuhiri (guests) to use te reo Māori in other contexts. Teacher-researchers in the A'oga Fa'a Samoa found that the study encouraged more exchanges of stories about the children's metalinguistic activities. For example, children felt confident to guide their peers to use the correct pronunciation of Samoan, and understanding about road safety learned at the centre in Samoan was interpreted and shared at home. Some *fanau* spoke of a renewed pride in their children's correct use of Samoan. Learning stories written in Samoan took on a deeper significance for teachers and children and their family.

The value of languages was evident in work undertaken in Mangere Bridge Kindergarten to redraft their philosophy statement to foreground languages rather than just cultures. This was particularly valuable in an English-medium setting where English, as the priority language for learning and teaching in a centre, can mean that other languages may be overlooked/neglected, even where teachers still consider themselves inclusive of diverse cultures. The power of language for care and education, and as a tool for expressing ideas and feelings, was important for children and families. Symonds Street Early Childhood Centre's measure of additive bilingual communication was demonstrated when several boys felt comfortable playing using Japanese. They used their home language for more complex purposes such as meta-play activity, to direct each other's roles and actions and the 'script'. Code-switching (moving into English when necessary) was also a common accomplishment.

Nevertheless, diverse languages were often used for control/instructions or greetings only. All centres realised that they needed a greater range of language/phrases at their disposal to enhance children's participation and to model affirmation. The research prompted richer use of language in a variety of situations, which enabled all children to see languages as a more powerful resource for learning.

Exploration—mana aotūroa

As noted, the research process prompted richer use of languages in a variety of situations. Heritage/home languages were viewed as valuable resources for communication in all learning and teaching experiences by teachers, children and family, and whānau. Children also began to explore each other's languages and demonstrated a growing metalinguistic awareness, particularly evident in the examples from Mangere Bridge Kindergarten, such as a child asking about "Tongan vanilla" to match French vanilla ice-cream, and a child asking her family what languages people spoke in different places throughout Aotearoa New Zealand. Another child encouraged to share language and cultural arts in the centre created intricate mehendi designs within a drawing programme.

In the A'oga Fa'a Samoa two girls used Samoan to speak to each other in a teacher–child mat-time role play; one encouraged the other in the teacher role to read a story book in Samoan, but when adopting the friend role spoke in English to further explain her rationale and motivations. Where bi- or multilingual teachers were available in Symonds

Street Early Childhood Centre and shared a heritage/home language with children, deeper exploration of children's working theories were possible; for example, about how snow was made. In three of the four centres where teachers were bilingual, considerable transfer of ideas through exchanges from home to centre were possible. Monolingual teachers also demonstrated the value of these home funds of knowledge through sensitive documentation in portfolios—the most read books at Mangere Bridge Kindergarten.

Implications for teaching and learning

Across all four centres the teachers reflected on the research and made changes to teaching. The process of engaging in this study raised awareness/consciousness and prompted reflection on teaching practices with regard to children who were learning in more than one language and the value of bilingualism for learning. Discussion about the value of bilingualism served to open up pathways to complement many families' view that they were able to maintain their heritage/home languages.

Sociocultural perspectives of learning and teaching underpinning this book draw attention to paying purposeful and systematic attention to the language resources that children bring to the centre as their tools for learning and educational achievement. The communities of the Samoan-immersion and Māori-medium centres made use of their heritage/home language for every facet of education and care. Teacher-researchers at Te Puna Kōhungahunga noted that the centre was moving increasingly towards being totally immersed in te reo Māori. Similarly, the aspirations of family and whānau and teachers to maintain their heritage/home languages across generations by using it for learning in a range of communities became a collaborative goal alongside use of English in English-medium settings. At Symonds Street Early Childhood Centre the teacher-researchers, themselves experienced in settling into Aotearoa New Zealand society, sought to engage parents new to Aotearoa New Zealand and the centre in conversations about the resources they have to sustain and grow the heritage/home languages, both inside and outside the centre. At Mangere Bridge Kindergarten the study added a further layer to the monolingual teacher-researchers' critical reflection on the ways in which inclusion was enhanced and enacted. They worked to make all languages visible and accepted as a resource for learning. However, the findings also raised awareness of the complexity of diversity as all teachers became increasingly responsive to the multiple languages represented in their centres.

Teachers in every centre tried out verbal and non-verbal strategies that were valuable for sustaining the child's wellbeing while activating the child's language knowledge, skills and dispositions through the use of stories, songs and play experiences. In all centres protocols and regular routines often provided unexpected metalinguistic benefits. Exploring teachers' and families' language resources might open up a rich seam of resources and support, as Symonds Street Early Childhood Centre illustrated in their systematic inclusion of the art, music and stories that were available in the funds of knowledge from the communities. The study encouraged teacher-researchers to document the ways they met the many challenges and opportunities using an additive bilingual approach in their particular context. Several examples of the exciting plurilingual possibilities where children felt comfortable using their languages in play and formalised routines are recounted in the earlier chapters. Where children and families find authentic and meaningful use of a heritage/home language outside of the centre context, such as on the marae or in the *fale* of elders, the family's pride in the children's achievements is communicated to the child, raising the status of the language for learning and language learning—a credit view of being an emerging bilingual (Cummins, 2009; Cummins, Bismilla, Cohen, Giampapa, & Leoni, 2005; Kenner et al., 2008).[1]

Research implications

The research team drew on complementary skills, knowledge and experience to design and implement the project. The four core team members (the editors of this book) remained throughout the study from its inception. Other team members changed but remained committed and connected to the study's purposes and outcomes.

We used a mixed-methods approach for data gathering and analysis, as described in detail in Chapter 3. The research team found that this design was appropriate within and across the four diverse early childhood centres, yielding rich data on languages used, valued experiences and opportunities and challenges.

The research indicated that Observer XT had potential, but ideally requires clearer video recordings than those obtained in this project. It also suggests the need to use multiple recording devices at the same time to realise its potential for analysing in-depth any and all aspects of children's and teachers' play-based language interactions where children are free to move around an educational setting. Another limitation was that we had installed Observer XT on a desktop computer at the University of Auckland. If it had been installed on a laptop we would have been able to visit teacher-researchers and get further input on analyses on-site rather than having them visit the university. Given the complexity of the software and the laborious nature of coding and analysing even short data samples, an enormous amount of researcher / researcher-assistant time is required to use this tool effectively. However, our research team was impressed with the capabilities of the software and would likely use it in future projects.

Our research partnerships, and the length of the time spent in qualitative data gathering and collaborative analysis, meant we were able to move beyond typical previous findings about the aspirations of diverse families, which have indicated that parents send children to centres to learn the language that is the medium of instruction. Instead, the findings opened up awareness that heritage/home languages have multiple valued purposes and outcomes that are part of families' deeper aspirations for their children.

These are valuable insights into future research design, as the research team proposes that there is still work to be undertaken to engage rewardingly with notions of language diversity and enhance the experiences of families and children who learn in more than one language in Aotearoa New Zealand. We acknowledge that collaborative relationships, shared understanding of cultural values and languages, and connections with cultural communities were crucial in this research. At the commencement of the study the researchers already had some well-established collaborative links with the four partner centres, as recommended for collaborative, mixed-method research designs (Penuel, Fishman, Cheng, & Sabelli, 2011). Trustworthiness of the findings was enhanced by a partnership approach and respondent validation. During the process of the study combined gatherings of the four centres fostered a climate of collaborative reflection, inquiry and sharing of insights: among the teacher-researchers, with the research team and, on several occasions, with our reference/advisory group members. Discussions at these gatherings helped "develop local capacity by fostering cohesion among networks of local actors" (Penuel et al., 2011, p. 334).

Theoretical conclusions and implications

Empowering children to transfer heritage/home languages securely to the next generation and/or gain the cognitive, social and economic benefits that fluent bilinguals can access depends primarily upon the length of time and opportunity for emerging bilingual children to learn in their heritage/home languages. Research from the United Kingdom, Australia, Canada and the United States indicates that to set and achieve a goal for bilingualism also requires the use of additive bilingual approaches, resources that include the child's funds of knowledge from home, and collaborative relationships between families and whānau, teachers and children to work in a complementary way to achieve this goal (Baker, 2011, Cummins, 2009; Genesee, 2015; Jones-Diaz, 2014; Kenner, 2004; McCaffery & McFall-McCaffery, 2010).

This study provided an opportunity for teacher-researchers and family and whānau to explore deeper understanding of the experiences of children learning in more than one language in four distinct ECE settings in the Auckland region. Parents' views about bilingualism have been noted in recent research to be the single most important factor in a child's successful uptake of bilingualism as family members and parents convey to children (directly and indirectly) their values of bilingualism and the value of knowing languages (Chen, Kennedy, & Zhou, 2012).

The teacher-researchers recognised, along with the families and the children themselves, that the languages and funds of knowledge used at home or in a community are valuable resources for learning, and they spoke about their own strategies for and challenges faced in sustaining heritage/home languages. The study also permitted much closer attention to be paid to the challenges and opportunities that each centre and home offered for fostering learning in more than one language. This in turn gave teacher-researchers, family and whānau members—and often the children too—cause to enquire into how, when, where and with whom heritage/home languages and literacies were being used and could be used as powerful resources for identity negotiation and for increasing social, cognitive and communicative knowledge and literacies in two or more languages (Kenner & Ruby, 2012). The study endorsed the immense value of having an inclusion policy in ECE centres that directly addresses the languages and literacies children bring with them as the starting point for working in a responsive and reciprocal way for social justice (Cummins, 2001, 2009; May, 2012).

There were widespread concerns expressed by family members and teachers about the loss of heritage/home languages once children entered the education system in Aotearoa New Zealand. Where there may be a focus on English only, the heritage/home language, as one of the significant markers of identity, risks being lost. Researchers also agreed that the cognitive benefits of learning in two languages include an increase in children's metalinguistic and metacognitive processing. This, in turn, enhances cognitive structures in the brain that can help in more complex problem-solving strategies and cross-language transfer of knowledge (Barac, Bialystok, Castro, & Sanchez, 2014; Cummins, 2009; Garcia & Wei, 2014). Such heightened metalinguistic awareness was documented in the A'oga Fa'a Samoa, where all the teachers, fluent in Samoan, immersed the children in the Samoan language. Some children confidently code switched (Samoan and English) as they decided which language to use, with whom and when:

> Strong promotion of the minority language within the school and preschool contexts not only enables children to develop proficiency in that language but also to develop age-appropriate conceptual knowledge and social interaction skills. Language acts as a lifeline to children's social and conceptual worlds. (Cummins, 2009, p. 269)

Final thoughts

Strategies for learning in and through more than one language can be fostered through use of the practical aspects of children's language resources—practical resources being fundamental to the notion of funds of knowledge. Furthermore, while documenting and honouring each family's heritage, teachers also more explicitly recognised and drew on their own funds of knowledge, languages and literacies in ways that were noticed and valued by the families.

Funds of knowledge and metalinguistic knowledge are not the sole preserve of bilingual or plurilingual teachers and children. The benefits of plurilingual activities in the centres were acknowledged by many families, and appeared to serve all children as empowering opportunities to gain experiences of how to live in a way that is affirming the cultures of friends and families and to make the most of languages-rich environments. English-medium centres can in this way make use of children's total language resources for learning, where possible, for teaching. As teachers and families collaborated to include and extend children's linguistic repertoires and enhance cognitive power, the plurilingual offerings included recognising rich underlying learning processes and funds of knowledge that were brought into the curriculum by learners and teachers, and the message that all families can contribute to learning and teaching: "families should be part of the assessment and evaluation of the curriculum as well as of children's learning and development" (Ministry of Education, 1996, p. 30). When secure in their relationships, and able to explore their multiple identities, children can use their total language and literacy resources as bilinguals and plurilinguals. Children are then able to take up the challenges and opportunities of building an empowering and just curriculum with their peers, teachers, and family and whānau.

References

Baker, C. (2011). *Foundations of bilingualism and bilingual education* (5th ed.). Clevedon, UK: Multilingual Matters.

Barac, R., Bialystok, E., Castro, D., & Sanchez, M. (2014). The cognitive development of young dual language learners: A critical review. *Early Child Research Quarterly, 29*(4), 699–714. doi: 10.1016/j.ecresq.2014.02.003

Chen, S. H., Kennedy, M., & Zhou, Q. (2012). Parents' expression and discussion of emotion in the multilingual family: Does language matter? *Perspectives in Psychological Science, 7*(4), 365–383.

Cummins, J. (2001). *Negotiating identities: Education for empowerment in a diverse society* (2nd ed.). Los Angeles, CA: Association for Bilingual Education.

Cummins, J. (2009). Pedagogies of choice: Challenging coercive relations of power in classrooms and communities. *International Journal of Bilingual Education and Bilingualism*, *12*(30), 261–271. doi: 10.1080/136700509/03003751

Cummins, J., Bismilla, V., Cohen, S., Giampapa, F., & Leoni, L. (2005). Timelines and lifelines: Rethinking literacy instruction in multilingual classrooms. *Orbit*, *36*(1), 22–26.

García, O., & Wei, L. (2014). *Translanguaging: Language, bilingualism and education*. New York, NY: Palgrave MacMillan.

Genesee, F. (2015). Myths about early childhood bilingualism. *Canadian Psychology/Psychologie canadienne*, *56*(1), 6–15. doi: 10.1037/a0038599

Jones-Diaz, C. (2014). Languages and literacies in childhood bilingualism: Building on cultural and linguistic capital in early childhood education. In L. Arthur, J. Ashton, & B. Beecher (Eds.), *Diverse literacies in early childhood: A social justice approach* (pp. 106–125). Camberwell, VIC: Australian Council for Educational Research.

Kenner, C. (2004). *Becoming biliterate: Young children learning different writing systems*. Stoke on Trent, London, UK: Trentham Books.

Kenner, C., Gregory, E., Ruby, M., & Al-Azami, S. (2008). Bilingual learning for second and third generation children. *Language, Culture and Curriculum*, *21*(2), 120–137. doi: 10.2167/lcc370.0

Kenner, C., & Kress, G. (2003). The multisemiotic resources of biliterate children. *Journal of Early Childhood Literacy*, *3*(2), 179–202. doi: 10.1177/14687984030032004

Kenner, C., & Ruby, M. (2012). *Interconnecting worlds: Teacher partnerships for bilingual learning*. London, UK: Institute of Education Press.

May, S. (2012). *Language and minority rights: Ethnicity, nationalism and the politics of language* (2nd ed.). New York, NY: Routledge.

McCaffery, J., & McFall-McCaffery, J. (2010). O tatatou o aga'i i fea? / 'Oku tatu o ki fe? / Where are we heading?: Pacific languages in Aotearoa / New Zealand. *AlterNative Special Supplement Issue Ngaahi Lea 'a e Kakai Pasifiki: Endangered Pacific Languages and Cultures*, *6*(2), 86–121.

Ministry of Education. (1996). *Te whāriki: He whāriki mātauranga mō ngā mokopuna o Aotearoa: Early childhood curriculum*. Wellington: Learning Media. Retrieved from http://www.education.govt.nz/early-childhood/teaching-and-learning/ece-curriculum/

Moorfield, J. C. (2011). *Te aka: Māori-English, English-Māori dictionary and index* (3rd ed.). Auckland: Longmann / Pearson Education.

Penuel, W. R., Fishman, B. J., Cheng, B. H., & Sabelli, N. (2011). Organising research and development at the intersection of learning, implementation, and design. *Educational Researcher, 40*(7), 331–337. doi: 10.3102/0013189X11421826

Reedy, T. (2013). Tōku rangatiratanga nā te mana mātauranga: "Knowledge and power set me free...". In J. Nuttall (Ed.), *Weaving* Te Whāriki*: Aotearoa New Zealand's early childhood curriculum document in theory and practice* (2nd ed., pp. 35–53). Wellington: NZCER Press

Ritchie, J. (2008). Honouring Māori subjectivities within early childhood education in Aotearoa. *Contemporary Issues in Early Childhood, 9*(3), 202–210. doi: 10.2304/ciec.2008.9.3.202

Ritchie, J. (2013). *Te Whāriki* and the promise of early childhood care and education grounded in a commitment to Te Tiriti o Waitangi. In J. Nuttall (Ed.), *Weaving* Te Whāriki*: Aotearoa New Zealand's early childhood curriculum framework in theory and practice* (2nd ed., pp. 141–156). Wellington: NZCER Press.

Endnotes

1 Note: See Appendix A and Appendix B for some suggested examples of reflective questions for teachers of children who learn in more than one language.

Appendix A

'The child's questions': Questions for teachers of children who learn in more than one language

We propose that the findings of this research can potentially be linked to 'the child's questions' so that teachers can develop and evaluate their strategies when working with children who learn in more than one language. The original set of child's questions derived from research designed to establish a teaching stories structure for teachers to evaluate their practice across the strands of *Te Whāriki* (May & Podmore, 2000), with connections to the learning stories framework for assessing children's experiences (Carr, 2001).

In a follow-up action research study of learning and teaching stories by Carr, May and Podmore (2002), the simplified child's voice questions served as the questions that centre teachers and educators initially asked of themselves as they commenced a process of self-evaluation. Since then, teachers and writers have sometimes drawn on these questions; for example, when writing learning stories. Adapted from May and Podmore (2000, pp. 67–69), the full and simplified forms of child's questions are as follows.

Strand of Te Whāriki	The 'child's question' in its full form	The 'child's question' simplified
Belonging Mana whenua	Do you appreciate and understand my interests and abilities and those of my family?	Do you know me?
Wellbeing Mana atua	Do you meet my daily needs with care and sensitive consideration?	Can I trust you?
Exploration Mana aotūroa	Do you engage my mind, offer challenges and extend my world?	Will you let me fly?
Communication Mana reo	Do you invite me to communicate and respond to my own particular efforts?	Do you hear me?
Contribution Mana tangata	Do you encourage and facilitate my endeavours to be part of the wider group?	Is this place fair for us?

In this study of learning and teaching with children who learn in more than one language, teachers and researchers found considerable connections between each of the four ECE centres' key themes and the strands of *Te Whāriki*. Given these now established connections, the research team propose that the child's questions, in both their full and simplified forms, could offer teachers a framework for evaluating and changing their teaching interactions in relation to the use of languages.

The child's questions are consistent with the UNCRC. As noted in Chapter 1, the child's right to be heard and to express her/his views is specified in the UNCRC (Article 12). Drawing on the theoretical notion of funds of knowledge (González, Moll, & Amanti, 2005), teachers might ask themselves to what extent they enquire about, appreciate and understand a child's interests and abilities and those of her/his family (Belonging: mana whenua: Do you know me?). Or, enacting an additive approach to bilingualism, teachers might reflect on how they invite a child to communicate and how they create a space for, and respond to, the particular efforts of that child (Communication: mana reo: Do you hear me?).

References

Carr, M. (2001). *Assessment in early childhood settings: Learning stories.* London, UK: Sage.

Carr, M., May, H., & Podmore, V. N. (2002). Learning and teaching stories: Action research in early childhood in Aotearoa–New Zealand. *European Early Childhood Education Research Journal, 10*, 115–126. doi: 10.1080/13502930285208991

González, N., Moll, L. C., & Amanti, C. (2005). *Funds of knowledge: Theorizing practices in households, communities and classrooms.* Mahwah, NJ: Erlbaum.

May, H. & Podmore, V. N. (2000). 'Teaching stories': An approach to self-evaluation of early childhood programmes. *European Early Childhood Education Research Journal, 8*(1), 61–73. doi: 10.1080/13502930085208/491

Appendix B

Questions for teachers to support the learning of children who learn in more than one language

What *maps* for teaching and learning will you be taking with you as you pull your waka on to the shore? Some suggested further reflective questions for teachers, adapted from the work of Cummins, Bismilla, Cohen, Giampapa and Leoni (2005), might include:

- What languages and literacies, cultures and identities, funds of knowledge and beliefs about bi/multilingualism do you bring, and what professional funds of knowledge about bilingual development do you have in your pedagogical kete?

- Do you construct an image of all children as competent and confident: what image of the child are you contributing to the centre's philosophy and practices of inclusion and empowerment?

- Are your own and children's languages and literacies from heritage/home languages made explicit/visible in the enrolment, teaching, learning and assessment processes; and what implicit views and values about their heritage/home languages for learning are children acquiring through your everyday practices?

- Does your pedagogical approach accord equal status to heritage/home languages and English as tools for learning and teaching in Aotearoa New Zealand, such that the image of the child who is learning in more than one language is seen as an emerging bilingual who is intelligent, imaginative and linguistically able?

- In what ways are you orchestrating a space at the centre to enable all children to transfer concepts from one language to another for deep cognitive engagement and to make use of their heritage/home languages, English and te reo Māori to negotiate and invest their identities in their learning as they contribute to the curriculum?

- Are your relational practices with colleagues and families working in a collaborative and complementary way to enable you to build on the cultural and linguistic capital, and the funds of knowledge of all of children, the teachers and the communities served?

Reference

Cummins, J., Bismilla, V., Cohen, S., Giampapa, F., & Leoni, L. (2005). Timelines and lifelines: Rethinking literacy instruction in multilingual classrooms. *Orbit*, *36*(1), 22–26.

Acknowledgements

We warmly acknowledge:

- the children, families and teachers in our partner centres
- the teacher-researchers: Marama Young and Jasmine Castle (Te Puna Kōhungahunga); Ene Tapusoa and May Crichton (A'oga Fa'a Samoa); Thirumagal Anandh, Auemetua Lotomau and Ruwinaaz Subhani (Symonds Street ECE); Carol Hartley, Pat Rogers, Jemma Smith and Daniel Lovatt (Mangere Bridge Kindergarten)
- the research team members from the University of Auckland who contributed to the earlier stages of this research: Dr Diane Mara, Patisepa Tuafuti and Dr Jenny Lee
- the University of Auckland summer scholars who worked on transcribing, translating or collating and entering data: Tania Popata, Makerita Atonio and Nur Farahain Ab Ghani
- the members of our Teaching and Learning Research Initiative (TLRI) project's reference (advisory) group: John McCaffery, Dr Constanza Tolosa, Professor Stephen May, Warahi Paki (Faculty of Education and Social Work, University of Auckland); Associate Professor Gary Barkhuizen (School of Cultures, Languages and Linguistics, Faculty of Arts, University of Auckland); Christine Murray, Kim Wyborn (Auckland Kindergarten Association); Karen Liley (Te Puna Kōhungahunga); Jan Taouma (A'oga Fa'a Samoa); Emma Ritzema-Bain (Deputy Principal, Mangere Bridge School); Andrea Jamieson (Deputy Principal, Waterlea School, Mangere Bridge); Stephanie Anich, Jonathan Ramsay (Principals, Richmond Road School, Ponsonby); Cherie Boyd, Celeste Harrington (Early Childhood Centres Managers, University of Auckland); Rosi Fitzpatrick (Teuila Consultants: Pasifika consultant); Fiona He Kobain and Anu Mysore (early childhood centre leaders)
- funding provided by the TLRI
- the TLRI advisers to the project: Jenny Whatman and Josie Roberts
- the Auckland UniServices Ltd research contract managers
- the University of Auckland Human Participants Ethics Committee
- the Auckland Kindergarten Association Research Access and Ethics Committee
- Monica Bland, Faculty of Education and Social Work at the University of Auckland, who organised and managed literature and references (RefWorks), assisted with the preparation of presentations on the research, and edited and formatted a draft of this entire book
- David Ellis, NZCER Press, for helpful communication during the process of writing and publishing this book
- Ray Prebble for insightful editorial reviewing and copyediting.

Index

A

additive bilingualism 21–22, 71, 75, 102, 103, 108, 117, 118, 127
ako 81
alofa (love and commitment) 58, 59, 60, 76
Ambury Regional Farm Park 98
A'oga Fa'a Samoa 13, 34, 57–58, 60–62, 122, 123–24
    ethnicities 35, 36
    languages spoken in the centre and at home 36, 37, 39, 40, 62–66, 68, 69–71, 72, 73–75, 124, 125, 126, 130
    opportunities and challenges 73–75
    overarching values 58–60, 75–76
    philosophy statement 58
    valued experiences and outcomes 65–73
Asian languages
    census data 7
    use in ECE 9
Asian New Zealanders
    see also Chinese New Zealanders
    census data 6
Auckland Kindergarten Association 98
Auckland region 6
    bilingual teachers 17
    ethnicities 6
    languages spoken 7, 8, 30, 80
    super diversity 6, 8, 80

B

belonging (mana whenua) 4, 18, 119, 123, 134
A'oga Fa'a Samoa 123
    immigrants 53–54
    Mangere Bridge Kindergarten 102, 103, 109, 110, 111, 113, 123
    Symonds Street Early Childhood Centre 85, 123
    Te Puna Kōhungahunga 49, 123
Bharathidasan, *Inbath Thamizh* (Tamil song) 96–97
biculturalism 81
    Te Puna Kōhungahunga 46, 49
    Te Whāriki 4, 5, 37
bilingual education, definition 23
bilingualism
    additive 21–22, 71, 75, 102, 103, 108, 117, 118, 127
    A'oga Fa'a Samoa 58, 71, 73, 75
    benefits in early years 90, 105, 129, 130
    definition 23
    in ECE centres 17–18, 116–17, 118, 119–20, 124–25, 126, 136
    emerging 23, 129, 136
    and heritage/home language loss 93–95, 96, 106, 130
    Mangere Bridge Kindergarten 102, 103–04, 105–06, 107–13
    parents' views 9, 16, 17–19, 48, 50–52, 69, 73, 83–84, 85, 88, 94–95, 103–04, 105–06, 129
    sociocultural research 14
    subtractive 22
    Symonds Street Early Childhood Centre 82–84, 86, 88, 90, 91, 93–96, 125–26
    Te Puna Kōhungahunga 46, 48, 50, 51, 55

biliteracy, Te Puna Kōhungahunga 48, 50, 55
buddying 87

C

census data, ethnicity 6
Centres of Innovation (COIs) research 13, 14, 58
children's rights
   see also early childhood education (ECE)
   to be educated in heritage/home languages x
   in early childhood centres 15
   to express views 2
   Māori children's right to be educated in te reo Māori 15
   United Nations Convention on the Rights of the Child (UNCRC) x, 2, 15, 135
Chinese New Zealanders, parents' perspectives on home and ECE learning 18–19
communication (mana reo) 5, 119, 124–25, 134
contribution (mana tangata) 4, 81, 118–19, 123–24, 134
   Symonds Street Early Childhood Centre 87, 124
credit-based view of learning x, 13, 14, 19–22
culturally responsive pedagogies 17, 20, 31

D

deficit views of children x, 19–20

E

early childhood education (ECE)
   data collection 9
   disjuncture in children's home and ECE experiences 17–19, 21
   ethnicities of children 9
   languages spoken by children 8–9
   parents' expectations 16, 18–19
   participation policy goal 3–4
Early Learning Information system (ELI) 9
Early Years Teaching and Learning Research Initiative (TLRI) project 30–31, 58, 130–31
   the child's questions 134–35
   data analyses 33–34
   data generation tools and procedures 32–33
   definition of terms 22–24
   ethical considerations 35
   further questions for teachers 136–37
   implications for teaching and learning 126–27
   participants 34
   quantitative findings across partner centres 35–42
   research design 31–35, 127
   research implications 127–29
   research questions and objectives 24–25, 30–31
   theoretical conclusions and implications 129–30
empowerment (whakamana) 5, 12, 15, 17, 22, 117, 118, 119–20, 129, 131, 136
   A'oga Fa'a Samoa 59, 74
   Mangere Bridge Kindergarten 108, 109, 112
   Symonds Street Early Childhood Centre 85, 92
English medium, definition 24

ethnicity
  Aʻoga Faʻa Samoa 35, 36, 80
  census data 6
  ECE data 9
  Mangere Bridge Kindergarten 35, 36, 99
  Symonds Street Early Childhood Centre 35, 36
  Te Puna Kōhungahunga 35, 36
exploration (mana aotūroa) 119, 125–26, 134

F

faʻaaloalo (respect) 58, 59, 60, 76
families/whānau 5, 15, 121
  see also teacher–family/whānau partnerships
  disjuncture in children's home and ECE experiences 17–19, 21
  expectations of early childhood education (ECE) 16, 18–19
  funds of knowledge 20–21, 88–89, 90, 104, 112, 117, 118, 121, 126, 127, 129, 131
  perspectives on bilingualism 9, 16, 17–19, 48, 50–52, 69, 73, 83–84, 85, 88, 94–95, 103–04, 105–06, 129
  perspectives on heritage/home languages viii, 18–19, 92–93, 100–02, 103–04, 105, 106, 109, 113, 121, 126, 128
  whānau, definition 24
  whānau development 13
funds of knowledge 20–21, 75, 88–89, 90, 91, 96, 99, 104, 112, 117, 118, 120, 121, 126, 127, 129, 130–31, 135

H

heritage/home languages
  see also indigenous languages; and also specific languages, e.g. Samoan language
  additive bilingualism 21–22
  children's right to learn in x
  as a cornerstone 96–97
  definition 23
  in ECE centres 8–9, 15–16, 17–18, 21–22, 119–20, 125, 129–30, 136
  and empowerment 119–20
  importance for cognitive learning 14
  loss of ix, 93–95, 96, 100–01, 105, 130
  Mangere Bridge Kindergarten 101, 102–04, 108–10, 113–14
  need to use positively 70
  parents' perspectives viii, 18–19, 92–93, 100–02, 103–04, 105, 106, 109, 113, 121, 126, 128
  protection 3
  silenced in educational settings ix
  Symonds Street Early Childhood Centre 81, 82–84, 89–91, 92–93, 96
Hindi
  census data 7
  children's understanding 8
holistic development (kotahitanga) 5, 15, 66–69, 74, 76, 121–22
home/heritage languages *see* heritage/home languages
Human Behaviour Analysis Observer XT 12.5 32–33, 34, 38–42, 117, 128
Human Rights Commission 3

I

identity
  children and families, Mangere Bridge Kindergarten 102, 104–05, 108, 109, 110–11, 112, 113
  children and families, Symonds Street Early Childhood Centre 85–86, 90–91, 96
  ethnic 9
  importance to children's learning 4
  Māori 5, 50, 54
  Pasifika children 5, 13
  relationship to culture and language 2, 12, 15, 16, 17–18, 32, 104–05, 119–20, 129–30
  Samoan 66, 68, 74
immigrants and refugees
  creating a sense of belonging 53–54
  fostering of language ix, x
  parents' expectations of ECE 16, 18–19
indigenous languages
  see also heritage/home languages
  children's rights 15
  intergenerational transfer 2, 16
  and monolingual models ix
  protection 2
  revitalisation 116
  United Nations Declaration on the Rights of Indigeneous Peoples x, 1
intergenerational language transfer and relationships ix–x, 2, 16, 17, 18, 48, 64–65, 92, 93, 94, 101–02, 103, 105, 106, 124
Inventory of Communicative Acts— Abridged (INCA-A) 41–42

K

Ka Hikitia: Accelerating Success 2013–2017: The Māori Education Strategy 5
kaitiakitanga (guardianship) 49
kaupapa-based action 13, 46, 48, 50, 51, 53
kōhanga reo 13

L

language loss ix, 18, 22, 73, 93–95, 96, 100–01, 105
language rights x, 15
Languages in Aotearoa New Zealand (Royal Society of New Zealand) 3, 8
languages spoken in Aotearoa New Zealand
  see also heritage/home languages; te reo Māori; and other languages, e.g. Samoan language
  A'oga Fa'a Samoa 36, 37, 39, 40, 62–66, 68, 69–71, 72, 73–75, 124, 125, 126, 130
  census data 7
  information on children's understanding 8
  Mangere Bridge Kindergarten 36, 37, 39, 40–41, 99, 100–02, 107–14, 124–25, 126–27
  Symonds Street Early Childhood Centre 36, 37, 39, 40–41, 81, 82–84, 88–89, 90–91, 93–96, 125–26, 127
  Te Puna Kōhungahunga 36, 37, 38, 39, 40, 47–48, 124, 126
leadership development, Māori immersion centres 13
learning stories 134

lotu practices 66–67

M

mana, significance of 118–19
manaakiakitanga (to support, take care of) 49, 50, 51, 52
Mangere Bridge Kindergarten 34, 98–100, 120, 122–23
   environments and communities 105–06, 107
   ethnicities 35, 36, 99
   experiences and outcomes 102–06
   identities 102, 104–05, 108, 109, 110–11, 112, 113
   languages spoken in the centre and at home 36, 37, 39, 40–41, 99, 100–02, 107–14, 124–25, 126–27
   opportunities and challenges 107–13
   relationships 103–04, 107, 108
Mangere Mountain (Te Pane o Mataoho) 98, 108
Māori
   see also te reo Māori
   census data 6
   deficit views of children x, 19–20
   Ka Hikitia: Accelerating Success 2013–2017: The Māori Education Strategy 5
   tikanga Māori 3, 15, 23, 47, 50, 52, 53, 108
Māori Language Act 1987 3
Māori Language Commission 3
Māori-medium services 4, 21, 117–18
   see also kōhanga reo; Te Puna Kōhungahunga
   definition 23
mat time 32, 33, 34, 38, 39, 42, 43
   A'oga Fa'a Samoa 40, 61, 63, 125

Mangere Bridge Kindergarten 39, 40–41, 102, 108–10, 111, 123
Symonds Street Early Childhood Centre 39, 40–41
Te Puna Kōhungahunga 40, 51, 52, 53
te reo Māori spoken 39, 40, 41
Maungawhau hīkoi, Te Puna Kōhungahunga 51, 52, 53
medium of instruction, definition 23
multiculturalism 81, 86, 88–89, 90
multilingualism *see* plurilingualism

N

National Student Number (NSN) 9
New Zealand Bill of Rights Act 1990 3
New Zealand Curriculum for English-medium Teaching and Learning in Years 1–13 5
New Zealand Sign Language (NZSL) x, 3

O

Observer XT 12.5 32–33, 34, 38–42, 117, 128

P

participation in ECE
   children who learn in more than one language 4–5
   policy goal 3–4
partnerships 12–13
   see also teacher–family/whānau partnerships
Pasifika ECE
   see also Samoan-language immersion centres
   parents' expectations 16
   research priorities 13

Pasifika Education Plan 2013–2017 5
Pasifika languages
   see also Samoan language; Tongan language
   intergenerational transmission 16
   use in ECE 9, 109
Pasifika peoples
   census data 6
   deficit views of children x, 19–20
peʻapeʻa (propeller) metaphor 59, 60, 76
pepeha (saying or motto) 39, 51, 53, 54–55, 122
plurilingualism 5, 8, 17, 18, 21, 116–17, 118, 119–20, 124–25, 130–31
   awareness of children at Aʻoga Faʻa Samoa 71–72
   challenges 93–95
   definition 23
   Mangere Bridge Kindergarten 107–14, 126–27
   opportunities 89–93
   Symonds Street Early Childhood Centre 80, 82–84, 88–93, 94, 96, 125–26
   Te Puna Kōhungahunga 50
portfolios 46, 108, 110, 111–13, 120, 126
poutu model 59, 60, 76

R

R software package 33
relationships (ngā hononga) 5, 15, 120, 131
   Mangere Bridge Kindergarten 103–04, 107, 108, 120
   Symonds Street Early Childhood Centre 85–87, 120

Te Puna Kōhungahunga 15, 45–46, 49–50, 52, 54, 55
Richmond Road Primary School *see* Aʻoga Faʻa Samoa
Royal Society of New Zealand, *Languages in Aotearoa New Zealand* 3, 8

S

Samoan language
   at Aʻoga Faʻa Samoa 36, 37, 39, 40, 58, 62–65, 70–71, 72, 74, 75, 124, 130
   census data 7
   children's transfer from Aʻoga Faʻa Samoa to other contexts 72–73
   children's understanding 8
   parents' proficiency and views 62–66, 68, 69–70, 73–75, 124
   parents' value of power 69–71, 124
Samoan-language immersion centres
   see also Aʻoga Faʻa Samoa
   English-medium kindergarten in partnership with 13–14
   teaching strategies 13–14
   women's contribution 59–60
social justice 3–4, 18, 130
sociocultural approaches 14, 20, 31–32, 126
spirituality
   lotu practices 66–67
   wairuatanga 49, 51, 53
super diversity vii, 6, 8, 80
Symonds Street Early Childhood Centre 34, 79–80, 81–82, 120
   challenges 93–95
   children contributing and taking responsibility 87, 124
   context and philosophy 80–81

cultural environment 80, 81, 88–89, 90–91, 123
ethnicities 35, 36, 80
experiences and outcomes 84–89
languages spoken 36, 37, 39, 40–41, 81, 82–84, 88–89, 90–91, 93–96, 125–26, 127
opportunities 89–93
relationships and identities 85–87
wellbeing and belonging 85, 123

T

tangata whenuatanga (indigeneity, belongingness) 49, 51, 53
taonga (valued customs and posessions) 3, 124
taonga tuku iho (holistic transfer of knowledge and spirituality) 48
Tātaiako 49
tautua (service and responsibility) 58, 59, 60, 76
te ao Māori 49, 50
Te Hāpai Ō 49
Te Puna Kōhungahunga 34, 45–46, 122, 123–24
 ethnicities 35, 36
 key themes, questionnaire and focus group data 49–52
 languages spoken in the centre and at home 36, 37, 38, 39, 40, 47–48, 124, 126
 opportunities and challenges 52–55
 self-review 53–54
 valued experiences and outcomes 48–52
te reo Māori
 A'oga Fa'a Samoa 38
 decrease in speakers 7, 118

ECE centre teachers' proficiency 37–38, 47–48, 117
in ECE centres 39, 40, 41, 117, 124
Mangere Bridge Kindergarten 38, 108, 109, 117
Māori children's right to be educated in 15
Māori children's understanding 8
official language of Aotearoa New Zealand 3
parents' proficiency 47–48, 117
policy document goals 4–5
revitalisation priority 7, 8, 15
Symonds Street Early Childhood Centre 38, 40, 41, 92, 117
taonga 3, 124
Te Puna Kōhungahunga 36, 37, 38, 39, 40, 47–48, 124, 126
Te Whāriki Communication strand 5
use in ECE 9
Te Whāriki
 aspiration statement 86
 bicultural emphasis 4, 5, 37
 Mangere Bridge Kindergarten 102, 103
 principles 1, 4, 14–15, 66, 81, 103, 118, 119–22
 sociocultural influences 31–32
 strands 4–5, 81, 118–19, 122–26, 134, 135
 Te Puna Kōhungahunga 49
Te Whatu Pōkeha 49
teacher–family/whānau partnerships 14–19, 116, 129, 131, 136–37
 A'oga Fa'a Samoa 65–66, 74, 76
 Mangere Bridge Kindergarten 99, 102, 109, 111–13

Symonds Street Early Childhood
  Centre 80–81, 90–91
Te Puna Kōhungahunga 49, 52,
  53, 54, 55
tikanga Māori (Māori practices and
  principles) 3, 15, 23, 47, 50, 52,
  53, 108
Tongan language 61, 63, 68, 72, 81,
  102, 104, 106, 110
  census data 7
  children's understanding 8
transnationals
  definition 23
  University of Auckland students 80
Treaty of Waitangi (Te Tiriti o
  Waitangi) 3, 4, 81
tuakana/teina (mentorship) 49, 52,
  87, 124

U

United Nations
  Convention on the Rights of the
    Child (UNCRC) x, 1, 2, 15, 135
  Declaration on the Rights of
    Indigenous Peoples x, 1
University of Auckland *see* Symonds
  Street Early Childhood Centre

whānau *see* families/whānau
whanaungatanga (relationships) 15,
  45–46, 49–50, 52
women, contribution in Samoan
  language ECE centres 59–60

W

wairuatanga (spirituality) 49, 51, 53,
  122
wellbeing (mana atua) 118, 122–23,
  127, 134
  A'oga Fa'a Samoa 69, 122
  Mangere Bridge
    Kindergarten 122–23
  Symonds Street Early Childhood
    Centre 85, 123
  Te Puna Kōhungahunga 122

www.ingramcontent.com/pod-product-compliance
Lightning Source LLC
Chambersburg PA
CBHW080807300426
44114CB00020B/2859